THE POWER OF HOW TO TALK TO ANYONE

Practical Tips to Eliminate Social Anxiety, Overcome Shyness, Improve Personal & Professional Relationships and Create Genuine Connections Anytime, Anywhere

GRANITE SPARKS

CONTENTS

INTRODUCTION

You're at a gathering, surrounded by laughter and animated conversations. Yet, you find yourself at the edge of the room, clutching a drink as if it were a lifeline. You desire to join in, to share a story or a laugh, but the words get stuck somewhere between your mind and your lips. The anxiety creeps in, whispering that everyone else is more confident and charismatic. It's a moment we've all experienced that can feel isolating and frustrating.

This book is about transforming those moments of anxiety into opportunities for connection. It's about moving from the sidelines to the center, not through sheer willpower, but with practical steps and genuine understanding. Imagine approaching a conversation with ease, knowing that you can express yourself clearly and connect with others meaningfully. This journey is not just about talking; it's about building bridges to more profound personal and professional relationships.

My name is Granite Sparks, and I've spent years helping adults overcome social anxiety and shyness. My passion lies in guiding others to find their voice and create genuine connections. I've seen firsthand how transformative communication can be. Whether through my workshops, personal experiences, or research, my insights aim to empower you with tools that work.

Social anxiety is more common than many realize. Studies strongly suggest that a significant portion of adults experience social anxiety at some point in their lives. It's not just an individual struggle. It's a shared challenge that affects personal happiness and professional success. Recognizing this widespread issue is the first step in addressing it.

The benefits of effective communication are vast. Imagine confidently walking into a room, knowing you can engage anyone in conversation. Visualize the impact on your relationships, deepening connections with friends and family. Consider the professional doors that open when you can express your ideas clearly and confidently. These are not distant dreams; they are achievable realities.

You may have tried to improve your communication skills before. Perhaps you've read other books or attended seminars that promised change but left you feeling the same. This book is different. It offers unique strategies that are practical and proven to be effective. They have worked for others, and they can work for you.

The chapters in this book are designed to guide you step by step. We will explore nonverbal communication, the silent language that speaks volumes. You'll learn the art of active listening, a skill that transforms conversations. We'll tackle difficult conversations and show you how to handle them gracefully. And we'll delve into building charisma, that elusive quality that draws people to you.

This is not just a book of ideas; it's a workbook of actionable content. Each chapter includes tips and exercises you can apply immediately. These are real-world applications designed for real people living real lives.

I encourage you to commit to this journey. Change requires effort, and the rewards are worth it. Be open to the process. Practice the skills. Your willingness to grow will make all the difference.

As you turn the pages, remember this: you have the power to transform your interactions. You can move from anxiety to confidence, from isolation to connection. This journey is yours to take, and it begins now. Let's start transforming those anxious moments into opportunities for meaningful connection. The adventure awaits.

CHAPTER 1

FOUNDATIONS OF EFFECTIVE COMMUNICATION

There's a moment many of us have faced: standing in a room full of people, feeling the weight of unsaid words, and wishing for the courage to speak up. It's the kind of experience that leaves you questioning your abilities, wondering if you're destined to always watch from the sidelines. But what if I told you that this feeling isn't permanent and that change is entirely possible? This chapter is about laying the groundwork for that change. It's about understanding the fundamental components of effective communication and realizing that you can transform how you interact with the world around you with the right mindset and tools. The foundation of effective communication is not just about talking; it's about understanding, connecting, and engaging in a way that feels authentic and empowering. This chapter will walk you through the essential elements, starting with the mindset that shapes everything else.

EMBRACING THE COMMUNICATION MINDSET

Adopting a growth mindset can be a game-changer for your communication skills. Developed by Stanford psychologist Carol Dweck, a growth mindset is the belief that abilities (including how we communicate) can be developed with time and effort. It's about seeing challenges not as insurmountable obstacles but as opportunities for growth and learning. When you encounter an awkward conversation or a meeting where you stumble over your words, a growth mindset encourages you to view these experiences as valuable learning opportunities. Instead of retreating into self-doubt, you begin to understand that each interaction is a chance to improve and refine your skills. Resilience becomes your ally, allowing you to bounce back from communication setbacks with a renewed determination to do better next time. This shift in perspective is crucial because it transforms failures into stepping stones rather than roadblocks.

Cultivating a positive attitude is equally important. You may wonder how optimism and openness can make a difference in your interactions. The answer lies in their transformative power. When you approach conversations with a positive outlook, you create an environment that invites connection and trust. Optimism encourages you to see potential rather than pitfalls, fostering a sense of curiosity that enriches your dialogues. Curiosity, after all, is the spark that ignites meaningful conversations. It drives you to ask questions, to learn about others, and to explore new ideas. By cultivating a mindset of openness and positivity, you open the door to richer, more fulfilling interactions. Techniques for maintaining this outlook can include daily affirmations, mindfulness practices, and surrounding yourself with positive influences that reinforce your commitment to growth.

Recognizing the impact of your beliefs is another critical component. Our beliefs about ourselves and others shape how we communicate, often in ways we don't immediately realize. This can become a self-fulfilling prophecy if you believe you're not a good communicator. You might inadvertently behave in ways confirming this belief, such as avoiding conversations or speaking hesitantly. By identifying and challenging these limiting beliefs, you can start to rewrite the narrative. Believe that you can grow and change, and your actions will begin to reflect this new belief. Your interactions will become more confident, more open, and more engaging.

Commitment to continuous improvement is the final piece of this puzzle. Communication is not a skill you perfect overnight; it's an ongoing process that requires dedication and practice. Developing a personal communication improvement plan can help you stay focused and motivated. Set specific goals for yourself, whether it's initiating more conversations, practicing active listening, or refining your nonverbal cues. Regularly assess your progress and seek feedback from others to gain insight into how you're doing. Remember, improvement doesn't happen in isolation. It requires a willingness to learn from every interaction and an openness to adapt as you grow.

Reflection Exercise: Identifying Limiting Beliefs

Take a moment to reflect on your limiting beliefs about your communication skills. Write them down, and then challenge each belief by writing a positive affirmation next to it. For example, if you believe, "I'm not good at public speaking," counter it with, "I am becoming a more confident public speaker with each opportunity I take." Use this exercise to transform your mindset and prepare yourself for future growth.

UNDERSTANDING SELF-AWARENESS IN INTERACTIONS

Self-awareness is the cornerstone of effective communication. It begins with a clear understanding of your unique communication style. This involves reflecting on your natural tendencies during interactions—do you often find yourself dominating conversations, or do you tend to hold back, letting others lead? Understanding these patterns is crucial. Take a moment to recall your last few conversations. Were there instances where you felt misunderstood or perhaps not heard at all? These reflections are invaluable. Consider conducting self-assessment exercises where you note not only your strengths, but also areas where you realize improvement is needed. This process allows you to view your communication habits objectively. You might also reach out to trusted peers for feedback. Ask them to share their honest perceptions of your communication style. What do they think you excel at? Where do they see room for growth? This external perspective can provide insights you might overlook on your own.

Emotional triggers can significantly hinder your ability to communicate effectively. These triggers often manifest as sudden feelings of anger, frustration, or anxiety during conversations. Perhaps someone interrupts you, and you feel dismissed, or you encounter a topic that makes you uncomfortable. Identifying these triggers is essential because they can derail interactions if left unchecked. Start by journaling your emotional reactions during conversations. Whenever you notice a strong emotion, jot down the context and your response. Over time, patterns will emerge, revealing specific situations or topics that provoke strong reactions. Understanding these triggers allows you to prepare for them, reducing their impact on your communication.

Enhancing emotional regulation is about managing these reactions so they don't control your interactions. Techniques such as deep breathing can be incredibly effective. Before entering a potentially stressful conversation, take a few deep breaths, inhaling slowly through your nose and exhaling through your mouth. This simple act can calm your nervous system, helping you maintain composure. Visualization exercises can also be beneficial. Take a moment to picture the interaction going smoothly, where you express yourself clearly and respond thoughtfully. This mental rehearsal can set a positive tone, making it easier to remain composed when a real conversation occurs.

While self-awareness often highlights areas for improvement, it's equally important to leverage your strengths. Are you naturally empathetic and able to connect with others on a deep level? Use this skill to build rapport and understanding. At the same time, recognize areas that need work. For those who tend to talk too much, practice active listening by focusing on what the other person is saying rather than planning your next comment. If you find yourself too reticent, challenge yourself to contribute one meaningful insight or question in each conversation. This balance of recognizing strengths while addressing weaknesses creates a more dynamic and effective communication style.

Exercise: Emotional Triggers and Strengths

1. **Identify Triggers:** Spend a week noting moments when you felt a strong emotional reaction during conversations. What were the circumstances? How did you respond?
2. **Reflect on Strengths:** List your top three communication strengths. How can you use these more effectively in your interactions?
3. **Plan for Improvement:** Choose one area you want to improve. Develop a strategy to address it in your subsequent conversations. For instance, if verbosity is your challenge, commit to summarizing your thoughts more concisely.

By integrating these practices, you'll find that self-awareness enhances communication and enriches relationships, fostering a more profound connection with those around you.

AUTHENTICITY OVER SUPERFICIALITY

Authenticity is more than just a buzzword; it's a powerful tool that underpins meaningful communication. When you speak from a place of truth, you invite others to connect with the real you, fostering trust and more profound relationships. Imagine sitting across from someone who shares their thoughts and genuine feelings. Their openness creates a safe space where honesty flourishes and connection thrives.

Authentic communication dismantles walls, allowing conversations to transcend superficial topics and explore the richness of shared experiences. This vulnerability, rather than displaying weakness, showcases strength. It signals a willingness to engage honestly, which in turn encourages others to do the same. The bonds formed through authenticity are resilient and capable of weathering misunderstandings and disagreements because they are built on a foundation of trust and mutual respect.

However, the line between being genuine and oversharing can be delicate. While authenticity invites connection, oversharing can alienate and overwhelm. It's important to balance honesty with privacy, ensuring that what you share is appropriate and constructive. Consider sharing personal information like seasoning a dish—just enough to enhance the flavor without overpowering it. Ask yourself why you're sharing a particular detail; is it to build a connection, or is it an attempt to seek validation or sympathy? By pausing to reflect on your intentions, you guard against the pitfalls of oversharing. This practice ensures that your interactions remain meaningful and respectful, maintaining the trust you've worked to build.

You must first find your inner voice to develop an authentic communication style. This involves identifying your core values and beliefs, the guiding principles that shape your interactions. Take time to reflect on what matters most to you in conversations. Is it honesty, empathy, or perhaps humor? Once you've identified these values, strive to embody them in your interactions. This might mean listening more deeply, speaking with kindness, or adding a touch of humor when appropriate. Authenticity doesn't require you to bear your soul in every conversation but calls for consistency between your words and actions. When your communication aligns with your values, you project sincerity that others can sense.

Manipulative techniques may seem like shortcuts to achieving desired outcomes in conversations but ultimately undermine trust and authenticity. Such tactics include feigned interest, exaggeration, or emotional manipulation to sway opinions or gain favor. While they might offer short-term gains, the long-term effects are damaging. Relationships built on manipulation are fragile, quickly crumbling under scrutiny. They breed suspicion rather than trust, leading to connections that seem more transactional than genuine. Instead, focus on sincerity. Speak and act in ways that reflect your true intentions. Authenticity doesn't just benefit others; it also enriches your own experience, allowing you to engage more fully and freely in every interaction.

Exercise: Finding Your Authentic Voice

Reflect on a recent conversation where you truly felt yourself. Jot down what made that interaction feel genuine. Was it the topic, the person, or your emotional state? Now, identify a conversation that felt forced or inauthentic. Consider what contributed to this feeling. Use these reflections to pinpoint your communication values and guide future interactions. Aim to incorporate these values consistently, allowing your authentic voice to shine through.

Embracing authenticity unlocks the potential for deeper, more fulfilling connections. You create a space where honesty is met with appreciation and where relationships can flourish without the weight of pretense.

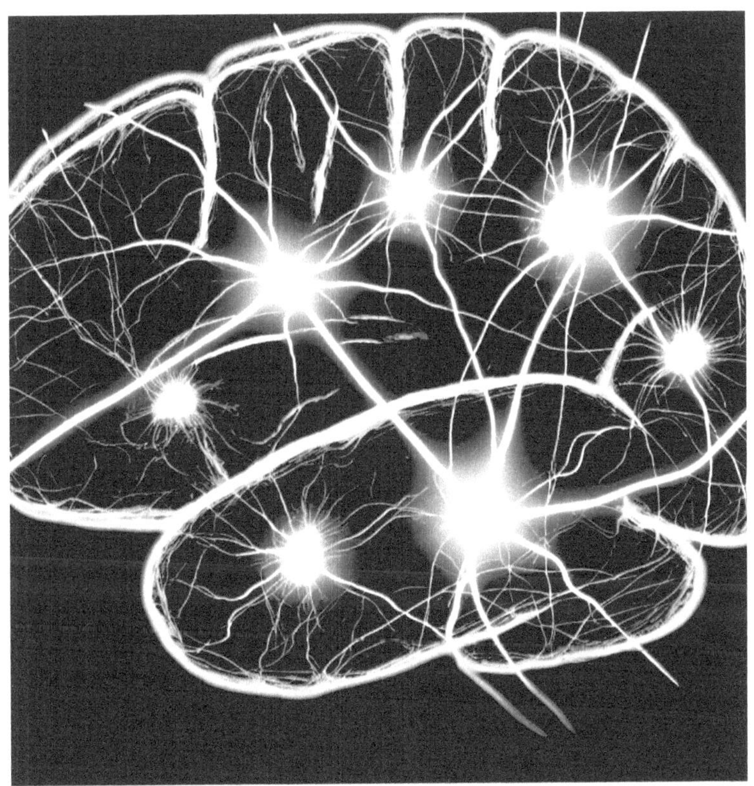

THE NEUROSCIENCE OF COMMUNICATION

Understanding the brain's role in communication unveils a fascinating world of biological processes that impact how we connect with others. At the heart of this exploration is the concept of mirror neurons, which play a pivotal role in empathy. These neurons, located in various parts of the brain, activate when we perform an action and when we observe someone else performing the same action. Picture yourself watching a friend smile as they recount a joyful memory; your mirror neurons fire, mirroring their happiness and creating a shared emotional experience. This neural mirroring allows us to empathize deeply and to feel what others feel, aiding in genuine connection. This connection isn't just a symbolic construct; it's a tangible process occurring in our brains, fostering understanding and emotional resonance.

Another crucial player in our communicative journey is the amygdala, a small, almond-shaped cluster of nuclei nestled deep within the brain. The amygdala is responsible for processing emotions, particularly those related to fear. Imagine you're about to speak in public, and suddenly, your heart races, your palms sweat, and your mind blanks. That's the amygdala at work, triggering a fear response. But understanding this can help you manage these reactions. Practicing mindfulness and deep breathing can calm the amygdala, allowing for more straightforward communication even in high-pressure situations. This awareness transforms fear from a paralyzing force into a manageable sensation, enabling you to engage confidently.

Neuroscience also offers insights into improving listening skills, which are crucial for effective communication. Our auditory processing abilities can be enhanced through deliberate practice and techniques. Consider the benefits of active listening exercises that train your brain to focus on the nuances of speech, such as tone and rhythm. By consciously engaging your auditory cortex, you sharpen your ability to process and understand spoken words, leading to more meaningful interactions. This focus on auditory processing extends beyond mere hearing; it involves truly absorbing and interpreting the speaker's intent and emotions, creating a space for attentive and empathetic dialogue.

The influence of dopamine in conversations is another intriguing aspect. Dopamine, often dubbed the "feel-good" neurotransmitter, plays a significant role in rewarding positive interactions. When you share a laugh with a colleague or have a heartfelt conversation with a friend, dopamine is released, reinforcing the pleasure of social bonding. This chemical reaction encourages us to seek out more of these positive experiences. To harness this effect, aim to create environments where uplifting interactions can flourish. Simple acts like expressing genuine gratitude, sharing compliments, or listening with intent can stimulate dopamine release, enriching your relationships and paving the way for deeper connections.

Stress responses managed through understanding brain function, are pivotal in maintaining effective communication under pressure. Stress often triggers the fight-or-flight response, clouding judgment and hindering clear expression. However, techniques such as progressive muscle relaxation and visualization can counteract these effects. Picture yourself in a serene setting, focusing on each breath as you progressively relax your muscles. This practice lowers stress hormones, allowing your brain to transition from a state of anxiety to one of calmness. Implementing these strategies creates a mental space where thoughts are coherent, and words flow more effortlessly, even in challenging scenarios.

Exercise: Enhancing Empathy Through Mirror Neurons

1. **Observe and Reflect:** Spend a day intentionally observing others' emotional expressions—whether in person or through media. Notice your emotional responses to these expressions.
2. **Mirror Back:** Practice mirroring these emotions in a controlled setting, such as with a friend or family member. Reflect on how this mirroring builds empathy and connection.
3. **Discuss:** Share your experiences with a friend, discussing how you felt and what you learned about empathy and connection through this practice.

This exercise helps you actively engage your mirror neurons, enhancing your ability to empathize and connect. By understanding and leveraging the brain's capabilities, you enrich your interactions, making communication an exchange of words and a shared human experience.

OVERCOMING FEAR OF REJECTION

Rejection. Even the word itself can send a shiver down your spine, evoking memories of missed opportunities or awkward encounters. It's a universal experience, yet the fear of it can feel intensely personal, seeping into our communication and reshaping how we interact with others. This fear often originates from a desire to belong, to be accepted and valued. Consider a scenario where you hesitate to join a conversation at a party, fearing that your contributions might be met with disinterest or dismissal. Those feelings of inadequacy stem from experiences and societal pressures, embedding deep-rooted anxiety about being turned away. Understanding where this fear comes from is the first step in dismantling its influence on you.

Building resilience to rejection transforms it from a daunting specter into a natural part of life. Think of rejection as life's way of guiding you toward environments and relationships that are more fitting. This perspective shift doesn't happen overnight, but with practice, it becomes easier. One effective strategy is to engage in rejection therapy, which involves intentionally putting yourself in situations where rejection is possible. Start small by asking for a discount where it's unlikely to be granted, or initiating a chat with someone outside your usual social circle. Over time, you'll notice a change in how you perceive rejection—less as a personal failure and more as a stepping stone to growth. Many successful individuals have faced rejection countless times, yet they persisted. Their stories remind us that rejection is not an end but a redirection. A person overcoming an obstacle, representing resilience in communication.

Reframing rejection is a powerful tool. Instead of viewing it as a verdict on your worth or abilities, see it as feedback. This cognitive shift allows you to extract valuable lessons from each experience. Ask yourself: what can I learn from this? How can I improve? Analyzing rejection through this lens transforms it into a constructive force that fuels your development. Cognitive reframing techniques encourage you to identify negative thoughts and replace them with more positive, realistic ones. This practice builds a mindset resilient to the sting of rejection, empowering you to move forward with renewed confidence.

Positive reinforcement plays a crucial role in combating fear. By nurturing a habit of positive self-talk, you foster a supportive inner dialogue that bolsters your confidence. Daily affirmations are a simple yet effective way to rewire your mindset. Begin each day by stating affirmations that resonate with you, such as "I am capable of handling whatever comes my way" or "Rejection is a sign of growth, not failure." These affirmations act as mental anchors, grounding you in positivity and resilience. Over time, this practice cultivates a mindset that not only withstands rejection but thrives in the face of it.

As you internalize these strategies, remember that overcoming the fear of rejection is a gradual process. Each step you take, no matter how small, is a victory. With each experience, you become more adept at navigating the complexities of human connection, turning potential rejection into a catalyst for growth. Embrace the journey, knowing that with each attempt, you are building a foundation of confidence and resilience that will serve you well in all facets of life. Doing so opens the door to richer, more meaningful interactions, free from the shackles of fear.

CHAPTER 2

MASTERING NONVERBAL CUES

Imagine you're in a lively café, meeting someone for the first time. As you navigate the conversation, you suddenly become aware of the subtle cues that paint the canvas of your interaction. From the gentle nods to the posture you both maintain, these nonverbal signals whisper the unspoken language of connection. Nonverbal communication crafts a narrative as vibrant and intricate as any spoken tale. Research suggests that much of our communication is nonverbal, encompassing gestures, postures, and space dynamics. As we explore these silent dialogues, you'll discover how to unlock the power of body language to forge authentic connections and easily convey confidence.

DECODING BODY LANGUAGE

Posture is the silent ambassador of your intentions, subtly communicating openness or defensiveness before words are even exchanged. Consider a moment when someone stood before you with open arms, uncrossed and relaxed. Their posture likely conveyed warmth, inviting you into their space with ease and approachability. Open postures like these signal receptiveness, creating an environment where dialogue flows freely. In contrast, closed postures—arms crossed tightly over the chest or a hunched stance—can unintentionally communicate defensiveness or discomfort. Such closed-off body language often acts as a barrier, signaling to others that you might not be fully engaged or open to interaction. By paying attention to your posture, you can consciously choose to project openness, paving the way for more meaningful exchanges.

Hand and arm movements are integral to our communicative toolkit, often revealing more than spoken words. When someone places their hands on their hips, it can denote confidence, perhaps even authority, suggesting they feel in control of the situation. Conversely, hands tucked in pockets imply shyness or a desire to retreat from the spotlight. The positioning of your hands can subtly influence how others perceive you, offering clues to your emotional state or intentions. Consider how a simple gesture, like extending an open hand when speaking, can reinforce transparency and honesty. Dominant gestures, such as expansive arm movements, signal assertiveness, while more subdued gestures communicate calmness. By becoming attuned to these signals, you can navigate conversations with a more in-depth understanding of the dynamics at play.

Mirroring behavior is a fascinating phenomenon where individuals unconsciously mimic each other's body language, fostering a sense of empathy and rapport. This natural mirroring often occurs between people who share a strong connection or mutual understanding. Imagine sitting across from a friend, noticing how you both lean in simultaneously or cross your legs in unison. This subtle dance of mimicry builds a bridge of familiarity, signaling that you are in sync with one another. By consciously mirroring the body language of others, you can enhance rapport, making interactions feel more harmonious and engaging. However, it's essential to approach mirroring with authenticity, ensuring it comes naturally rather than feeling forced or contrived.

Personal space dynamics play a crucial role in how comfortable interactions feel. Each culture has its own set of norms regarding personal space, influencing how close or distant we stand from others. In some cultures, close proximity is a sign of trust and intimacy; in others, it might be perceived as intrusive. If you've ever felt the discomfort of someone standing too close, you understand how personal space can impact interactions. Recognizing these subtle yet powerful cues allows you to navigate social situations with greater sensitivity and awareness. By respecting personal space, you demonstrate attentiveness to the comfort levels of those around you, fostering an environment of mutual respect and understanding.

Exercise: Personal Space Reflection

Take a moment to observe your own personal space preferences. Think about situations where you felt either comfortable or uncomfortable due to proximity. Reflect on how these experiences have shaped your interactions. Consider journaling these observations, noting any cultural influences or personal tendencies. This reflection can enhance your awareness of personal space dynamics, enabling you to adapt more effectively in diverse social settings.

Embracing the nuances of nonverbal communication empowers you to connect with others on a deeper level, transcending the barriers of spoken language. As you tune into these silent signals, you'll discover a world of rich interaction, where every gesture, posture, and glance contributes to the symphony of human connection.

FACIAL EXPRESSIONS AND THEIR IMPACT

Facial expressions are a universal language that transcends borders and cultures, providing a window into our emotions. Imagine a friend across the table, their face lighting up with a smile that instantly lifts your mood. Or think of the furrowed brows and downturned lips that unmistakably convey sadness or concern. These expressions are rooted in our biology, representing the six basic emotions recognized globally: happiness, sadness, fear, disgust, anger, and surprise. Each emotion carries its own distinct facial signature, etched into our expressions and instantly recognizable to others. This recognition is not just cultural; it's an innate human trait that connects us all. Understanding these universal signals can enhance your ability to communicate effectively and empathetically, allowing you to navigate interactions with a deeper awareness of the conveyed emotions.

Among these expressions, the smile holds a special place as a powerful tool for connection. But not all smiles are created equal. The Duchenne smile, named after the French neurologist who identified it, is characterized by the crinkling of the eyes, an involuntary movement that signals genuine joy. This smile is authentic, radiating warmth and sincerity. In contrast, a polite or forced smile lacks these eye crinkles, revealing a more controlled, less heartfelt emotion. This distinction is crucial when building trust and rapport, as genuine smiles foster genuine connections. By learning to spot the difference, you can better interpret the emotions of those around you, responding with empathy and understanding. This awareness strengthens personal bonds and enhances professional interactions, where sincerity is often the key to successful collaboration.

The subtlety of microexpressions adds another layer to our understanding of facial cues. These fleeting expressions, lasting only a fraction of a second, reveal hidden emotions that people might not even be aware they're displaying. These microexpressions can be a goldmine of information, offering insights into genuine feelings beneath the surface of words. By training yourself to recognize these quick flashes of emotion, you can become more attuned to the unspoken truths in your interactions. To hone this skill, consider practicing in controlled settings, perhaps with a friend or through online resources. The ability to read microexpressions enhances your emotional intelligence and equips you with the ability to detect deception and navigate complex social landscapes with greater finesse.

Facial expressions do more than convey emotions; they also influence our emotional experience and how others perceive us. The facial feedback hypothesis suggests that forming a facial expression can affect our emotional state. For example, the simple act of smiling, even when you're not feeling particularly happy, can trigger the release of neurotransmitters like dopamine and serotonin, boosting your mood and increasing your approachability. This effect is not just internal; it radiates outward, affecting how others respond to you. A genuine smile makes you seem likable and trustworthy, encouraging others to open up and engage. This phenomenon underscores the power of facial expressions not just as communicative tools but as active participants in shaping the emotional dynamics of any interaction.

Reflection Section: The Impact of a Genuine Smile

Think about a recent interaction in which a genuine smile made a difference. What was the situation, and how did that smile change the atmosphere? Reflect on how you felt and how the other person might have perceived you. Consider keeping a journal to note these observations, which will help you become more aware of the power of your expressions and how they shape your interactions.

Understanding facial expressions enriches your communication toolkit, allowing you to engage more deeply and empathetically with the world around you. In a world where words often fall short, these silent signals speak volumes, guiding you through the intricate dance of human connection.

THE POWER OF EYE CONTACT

Consider the moment when your eyes meet someone else's across a room, and in that brief connection, an understanding forms a silent agreement to acknowledge one another. Eye contact is a powerful tool for building trust and engagement in interactions. It is an invisible thread weaving through conversation, holding attention, and conveying interest. In many Western cultures, direct eye contact signifies confidence and attentiveness. It tells the other person, "I am present and value this exchange." Yet, it's important to remember that cultural differences shape how eye contact is perceived. In some Asian cultures, for instance, direct eye contact can be seen as aggressive or disrespectful, highlighting the need for cultural sensitivity. Understanding these nuances ensures that eye contact fosters connection rather than causing discomfort.

Balancing eye contact is a delicate dance. Too much can feel intense, even intimidating, while too little might suggest disinterest or evasion. The key lies in finding a natural rhythm, where eye contact punctuates conversation instead of dominating it. Consider the "triangle gaze" technique, where your eyes gently move around the person's face, from eyes to mouth, creating a soft, engaging focus without staring. Breaking eye contact naturally is also essential, whether by glancing away to consider a thought or looking briefly to the side. These subtle shifts maintain engagement while providing moments of relief, ensuring the interaction remains comfortable for both parties.

Deliberate eye contact has the power to express genuine interest and attentiveness. Holding someone's gaze during a conversation signals that you are fully present and invested in what they have to say. This act of focus can transform an ordinary exchange into an intimate dialogue where the other person feels valued and understood. To sustain eye contact without discomfort, try the "60-40 rule": maintain eye contact about 60% of the time, allowing for natural breaks. This balance creates a sense of connection while respecting personal boundaries. The skillful use of eye contact can deepen relationships, turning fleeting encounters into meaningful interactions.

On the other hand, a lack of eye contact can reveal discomfort or dishonesty. When someone avoids your gaze, it might suggest they are hiding something or feeling uneasy. Patterns of eye movement can be particularly telling during moments of deception. For example, frequent shifts in gaze or looking down might indicate that someone is fabricating details or feeling anxious. By paying attention to these cues, you can gain insight into the emotional undercurrents of a conversation. However, it's essential to interpret these signals with care and context, as individual differences and cultural norms can influence eye contact behaviors.

Incorporating eye contact into your communication reper-
toire enriches your ability to connect authentically with
others. This powerful nonverbal cue transcends words,
allowing you to convey empathy, sincerity, and engagement.
As you navigate diverse interactions, remember that eye
contact is not just a tool but an invitation—a way of saying,
"I see you, and you matter."

GESTURES THAT ENHANCE CONNECTION

Gestures serve as a silent language, often speaking louder
than words ever could. They are the subtle punctuation
marks in our conversations, adding emphasis and emotion to
our stories. Take, for instance, the simple act of nodding. In
many cultures, a nod signifies agreement or understanding, a
silent affirmation that words alone may not fully capture.
Yet, in some parts of the world, like Greece or Turkey, a nod
might mean the opposite, signifying disagreement. Understanding these cultural nuances can prevent misinterpreta-
tions and smooth over potential miscommunications. The
handshake, another common gesture, varies in its significance across the globe. In Western cultures, a firm handshake is a sign of confidence, while in some Asian cultures, a
softer handshake is preferred, emphasizing respect and
humility. These gestures are not just movements but echoes
of cultural heritage and personal expression.

Refining your gestural communication involves more than
just knowing when to nod or shake hands. It's about using
gestures to complement your verbal messages, adding layers
of meaning to your words. Open-handed gestures, for exam-

ple, can indicate transparency and honesty, creating an atmosphere of trust. You invite openness and collaboration when you speak with your palms facing up. This simple yet powerful gesture can make others feel more comfortable and willing to engage in conversation. But beware of the pitfall of over-gesturing. Too many hand movements can distract from your message, drawing attention away from your words. Imagine a speaker whose hands flit about like birds, their message lost in the chaos of their gestures. Moderation is key. Your gestures should highlight your words, not overshadow them.

Adapting your gestures to different contexts is crucial for effective communication. What works in a casual setting may not be appropriate in a formal one. In a relaxed environment, you might use more animated gestures, your body language reflecting the informal nature of the conversation. However, such exuberance might be seen as unprofessional or distracting in a professional setting. Here, your gestures should be more restrained, and your movements should be deliberate and measured. This adaptability shows your awareness of the social landscape and your ability to read the room and adjust accordingly. It's a skill that can enhance your communication, making your interactions more meaningful and impactful.

Understanding the nuances of gestural communication can transform your interactions, turning simple conversations into rich exchanges of thoughts and feelings. It's about more than just what you say; it's about how you say it. Your gestures are an extension of your voice, a visual representation of your message. By becoming more aware of your gestures and their potential impact, you can ensure that your nonverbal communication aligns with your intentions. You create a congruent message where words and gestures harmonize to convey your thoughts and emotions. This alignment enhances your credibility, making your communication more persuasive and engaging.

Reflect on the gestures you use daily. Consider their impact on your interactions. Are they congruent with your words? Do they enhance or distract from your message? Paying attention to these details can refine your gestural communication, making it a powerful tool in your communicative arsenal. This awareness allows you to connect more deeply with others, fostering relationships built on understanding and mutual respect. It's a journey of self-discovery that opens up new possibilities for connection and growth. As you explore the world of gestures, remember that each movement is an opportunity to express yourself and to connect with others in a language that transcends words.

ALIGNING VERBAL AND NONVERBAL SIGNALS

Imagine telling a friend you're "fine" while your eyes are downcast and your lips form a tight line. This discrepancy between your words and body language creates confusion. When verbal and nonverbal cues don't align, they send mixed messages, leaving others unsure of your true feelings. This misalignment can unintentionally undermine your credibility and trustworthiness. It's like trying to listen to music with headphones, where each ear plays a different song. The result is noise, not harmony. Consistency in your communication is about ensuring that your words and body speak the same language. It involves an intentional awareness of how your gestures, expressions, and tone complement your verbal message, creating a coherent and powerful narrative.

A consistent alignment between verbal and nonverbal signals enhances clarity in communication. Think of it as a well-rehearsed dance, where each step is in sync with the music. This harmony allows your message to be received as intended, minimizing misunderstandings. When your body language reinforces your words, it amplifies your message, making it resonate with authenticity and sincerity. This alignment is crucial in sensitive conversations, where even a slight mismatch can lead to confusion or doubt. For instance, when offering support to a friend in distress, your comforting words should be accompanied by open, empathetic gestures that reflect genuine concern. This consistency ensures that your message is clear and your intentions are understood, fostering trust and connection.

Self-awareness of your nonverbal habits is vital in achieving this alignment. Begin by observing yourself during conversations. Consider how your body naturally reacts to different emotions or situations. Are your gestures often in sync with your words, or do they sometimes contradict your intended message? Self-monitoring techniques, such as recording and reviewing a conversation later, can be incredibly revealing. Pay attention to your posture, facial expressions, and hand movements. This exercise helps you identify patterns and areas where your nonverbal signals might need refinement. By becoming more aware of these habits, you gain control over your communication, allowing you to adjust and align your signals with your verbal content.

Recognizing and addressing misalignment in real-time interactions requires a keen sense of awareness and adaptability. Imagine you're passionately presenting an idea in a meeting, but your arms are crossed, and your eyes dart around the room. Such incongruence can dilute the impact of your message. To correct this, develop realignment techniques that enable you to adjust your cues on the fly. If you notice your body language becoming defensive or closed, consciously open your posture, relax your arms, and maintain steady eye contact. These adjustments can quickly bring your nonverbal signals back in line with your verbal message, reinforcing your credibility and ensuring your audience receives the intended message.

As you integrate these practices into your daily interactions, you'll find that your communication becomes more effective and engaging. Your words will carry greater weight, and your messages will resonate with clarity and conviction. This alignment enhances your interactions and strengthens your professional presence, allowing you to communicate with confidence and authority. By aligning your verbal and nonverbal signals, you create a power that elevates your communication to a new level of effectiveness.

In mastering these nonverbal cues and aligning them seamlessly with your spoken words, you unlock a new dimension of communication. It's not just about saying the right things; it's about embodying them, ensuring that every gesture and expression reinforces your message. This coherence fosters deeper connections, paving the way for genuine interactions that resonate with authenticity and empathy. As we move forward, we'll explore how these foundational skills can be applied to enhance your personal and professional relationships, creating a world where effective communication opens doors to limitless possibilities.

CHAPTER 3

BUILDING CONVERSATIONAL CONFIDENCE

Picture yourself at a networking event, surrounded by unfamiliar faces, each engaged in their own conversations. You're holding a drink, scanning the room, trying to find an opening to join in. The idea of starting a conversation seems daunting. What do you say? How do you break the ice without feeling awkward? These questions are common, and you're not alone in facing them. Many adults find themselves in similar situations, longing for the ease of engaging confidently with others. The good news is that conversational confidence can be cultivated and begins with mastering the art of the icebreaker.

Icebreakers are more than just conversation starters; they are bridges that connect strangers in a room. Their purpose is to ease tension, turning what could be a nerve-wracking experience into an inviting atmosphere. Consider a situation where you walk up to someone new and ask about their favorite book or recent travels. These questions aren't just fillers; they invite the other person to share a piece of their world with you. Icebreakers create a space where connection can blossom, setting the tone for meaningful dialogue. They encourage openness, breaking down barriers and paving the way for genuine interaction.

Crafting personalized icebreakers is an art that involves aligning the conversation starter with your personality and the context. For example, starting with a question about recent technological advancements can be engaging and relevant if you're at a tech conference. Shared interests often serve as fertile ground for conversation. Perhaps you notice someone wearing a band t-shirt you recognize. Asking about their favorite concert can lead to a lively exchange about music preferences. By tailoring your approach, you make the interaction feel natural and effortless, creating a memorable first impression.

Simple, neutral conversation openers are invaluable tools in your conversational toolkit. They are adaptable and suitable for almost any setting. Asking about the weather might seem trivial, but it's a universal topic everyone can relate to. Inquiries about the shared environment, such as the venue or event, provide common ground. These starters might seem basic, but they serve a critical function: they open the door to dialogue, allowing both parties to ease into the conversation gradually. As comfort levels rise, the discussion can naturally evolve into more substantial topics.

Humor can be a powerful ally in breaking the ice, but its use requires finesse. Light-hearted observations can inject a sense of fun into the interaction, making it more enjoyable for both parties. Imagine you notice a quirky piece of art on the wall and make a playful remark about it. Such humor can alleviate tension, providing a shared moment of levity. However, it's essential to gauge the other person's receptiveness. Self-deprecating humor, when used sparingly, can also be effective, as it shows humility and relatability. The key is to ensure the humor aligns with the context and feels authentic, not forced.

Exercise: Crafting Your Personalized Icebreakers

1. **Identify Your Contexts:** List the top three social settings you frequently find yourself in, such as work functions, social gatherings, or hobby-related meetups.

2. **Create Tailored Starters:** For each setting, create two personalized icebreakers that reflect your interests and the context. For example, at a work function, you might ask, "What project are you excited about this year?"

3. **Practice and Reflect:** Use these icebreakers in your subsequent interactions. Reflect on the response and refine your approach as needed.

As you experiment with these techniques, remember that building conversational confidence is a journey. Each interaction is an opportunity to learn and grow, bringing you closer to the ease and authenticity you seek in social exchanges.

STRATEGIES FOR OVERCOMING SHYNESS

Shyness can often feel like an invisible barrier, holding you back from expressing yourself freely in social situations. When tackling this challenge, it's crucial to understand where your shyness originates. Often, it stems from experiences that have shaped your self-perception. Perhaps a comment during your formative years made you question your worth, or maybe a social mishap left a lasting imprint on your confidence. Though seemingly small, these moments can accumulate over time, creating a narrative of self-doubt. By identifying these root causes, you can unravel the threads of shyness that have woven into your interactions. Reflecting on these experiences isn't about dwelling on the past but recognizing patterns to move forward with greater self-awareness and kindness toward yourself.

Gradual exposure techniques offer a gentle yet effective way to ease into social situations and build confidence. The idea is to start small, immersing yourself in familiar settings where you feel comfortable. This could be as simple as chatting with a trusted friend or participating in a small group discussion at work. As you become more at ease, gradually expand your comfort zone. Consider role-playing exercises with a supportive friend or family member. By simulating social interactions in a safe environment, you can practice responses and expressions, reducing anxiety when facing similar real-life situations. This step-by-step approach allows you to build resilience and confidence at your own pace, making the transition from shy observer to active participant feel less daunting.

Developing assertive communication skills is another powerful tool in overcoming shyness. Assertiveness isn't about being loud or domineering; it's about expressing your thoughts and feelings openly and respectfully. One effective technique is the use of "I" statements. Instead of saying, "You never listen to me," try, "I feel unheard when my opinions aren't considered." This subtle shift focuses on your feelings rather than blaming the other person, paving the way for constructive dialogue.

Additionally, setting personal boundaries is vital. Know your limits and communicate them clearly, whether you need time alone to recharge or prefer not to discuss certain topics. By asserting your needs, you create an environment where you feel respected and valued, reducing the fear of being overwhelmed or dismissed.

Visualization can also play a transformative role in boosting your confidence. Before entering a social scenario, take a few moments to visualize a positive outcome. Picture yourself engaging in a conversation with ease, your words flowing naturally. Imagine the smiles and nods of understanding from those you're speaking with. This mental rehearsal primes your brain for success, reducing anxiety and increasing your comfort level when the actual interaction occurs. Consider mentally rehearsing key phrases you might use, allowing you to feel more prepared and articulate. Visualization is a powerful practice that enables you to experience success internally before it manifests externally, reinforcing your belief in your ability to connect with others meaningfully.

TECHNIQUES FOR ENGAGING IN SMALL TALK

Small talk often feels like a necessary hurdle, a gateway to more meaningful connections. Getting stuck in the loop of exchanging pleasantries is easy without ever reaching a deeper understanding. However, the transition from small talk to substantial conversations can be seamless. One effective technique is to ask open-ended questions that invite more than a yes or no response. Instead of asking, "Did you enjoy the movie?" you might say, "What did you think of the movie's ending?" Such questions encourage elaboration, naturally allowing the conversation to delve into shared interests or perspectives. This approach can transform a superficial exchange into a dialogue rich with insight and engagement, opening doors to genuine connection.

Finding common ground is the cornerstone of any engaging conversation. It requires a keen sense of observation and a genuine interest in the other person. You can quickly establish rapport by making observational remarks about the environment or noting something specific about the person you're speaking with. For example, if you're at a party and notice someone wearing a t-shirt of a band you like, a comment like, "I love that band; have you seen them live?" can spark a conversation based on mutual interests. Discussing mutual acquaintances is another effective method to find common ground. Mentioning a shared friend or colleague can provide a familiar touchpoint that makes the interaction feel more personal and connected.

While small talk can be the starting point for deeper conversations, it has its pitfalls. One common mistake is monopolizing the conversation, turning it into a monologue rather than a dialogue. It's important to balance the exchange, allowing both parties to contribute. Another pitfall is sticking to safe, overly generic topics that need more engagement. Conversations that remain on the surface often need more depth to build a meaningful connection. By being mindful of these tendencies, you can steer the conversation toward more substantial topics that captivate and resonate with both parties.

Active listening is a critical component of effective small talk. It involves more than just hearing words; it's about truly understanding the speaker's intent and emotions. Nodding and offering verbal affirmations such as "I see" or "That's interesting" can show that you are engaged and present. Reflective listening techniques, where you paraphrase or summarize what the other person has said, further demonstrate your attentiveness. For instance, if someone shares a story about their recent travels, you might respond with, "It sounds like you had a great adventure in Italy." This validates the speaker's experience and keeps the conversation flowing, encouraging further sharing.

Reflection Section: Enhancing Your Small Talk Skills

Consider a recent conversation where small talk led to a deeper connection. Reflect on what made it successful. Was it a shared interest, an open-ended question, or a moment of active listening that turned the tide? Write down your observations and think about how you can apply these insights to future interactions. This practice of reflection can help you identify patterns and strategies that work for you, ultimately enhancing your conversational skills.

NAVIGATING AWKWARD SILENCES

We've all been there. You're conversing, and suddenly, silence falls like an unexpected curtain drop. Awkward silences are normal, yet they often feel uncomfortable, leaving you scrambling for what to say next. Understanding why these pauses occur is key to managing them. Sometimes, they happen because you're processing what a person is saying. Other times, it's a natural lull as the conversation shifts. Recognizing this can ease the pressure to fill every gap with words. Instead of fearing silence, consider it a natural part of communication. It's not an enemy but a space for thought and reflection.

Silences offer a unique opportunity to deepen conversations. Use them to reflect on what's been shared and think about how to respond meaningfully. This pause can be a chance to transition smoothly to new topics. If you find the conversation waning, consider asking a reflective question. For instance, if discussing a recent event, you might ask, "How did that experience change your perspective?" Such questions invite more profound thought and can reignite the dialogue. Embrace silence as a moment to gather your thoughts, ensuring that what you say next adds value to the exchange.

Developing skills for smooth transitions between topics helps you navigate conversations more fluidly. Think of it as a bridge that connects different parts of a dialogue. Bridging techniques involve linking what's just been discussed with a new topic. For example, if you're talking about a recent movie, you might pivot by saying, "That film reminded me of the book I'm currently reading. Have you read anything interesting lately?" This approach keeps the conversation dynamic and engaging. It's also about being adaptable, knowing when to shift gears, and exploring new avenues of discussion. Topic pivoting requires attentiveness and creativity, allowing the conversation to evolve naturally.

Maintaining composure during silences is crucial. Your body language can convey comfort and confidence, even when words are momentarily absent. A relaxed posture signals your ease, reassuring your conversation partner. Maintaining eye contact, even during pauses, shows you're engaged and attentive. It's a silent affirmation that you're present and invested in the conversation. Avoid fidgeting or looking away; these actions can suggest discomfort or disinterest. Instead, embrace the pause, using it as an opportunity to connect on a deeper level without the need for constant chatter. Your quiet composure and acceptance that silence is a part of the conversation will make you feel at peace during such lulls.

Navigating these moments requires a balance of calm and curiosity. It's about being present, not rushing to fill the void, but allowing the conversation to unfold at its own pace. Embrace the silence as a space for possibilities, where the next chapter of your interaction can begin.

BUILDING CONFIDENCE IN PROFESSIONAL SETTINGS

Navigating the professional world often demands more than just competence in your field; it requires a strategic approach to communication. Preparing for professional interactions starts with a foundation of mental readiness and strategic planning. Before heading into a meeting or networking event, take the time to research relevant topics. Understanding current trends and critical issues in your industry enhances your confidence and provides you with solid ground to contribute meaningfully to conversations. This preparation allows you to craft key talking points that can guide your interactions, ensuring you stay focused and articulate. Having a few well-thought-out points in your arsenal can help steer discussions, making your contributions relevant and impactful.

Your nonverbal cues speak volumes in professional settings, often conveying messages more powerfully than words. A firm handshake, for example, is not just a greeting; it's a statement of confidence and professionalism. When you extend your hand with assurance, you establish an immediate connection that can set the tone for the entire interaction. Similarly, professional attire and posture are pivotal in how you are perceived. Dressing appropriately for the occasion shows respect for the environment and the people you engage with. Meanwhile, maintaining an upright posture signals that you are attentive and engaged. These nonverbal signals collectively create an image of authority and confidence, encouraging others to view you as a credible and capable professional.

Building a professional network is a continuous journey that thrives on effective communication. Networking skills can transform initial meetings into valuable connections. Crafting a concise and compelling elevator pitch is a skill worth honing. This brief introduction should encapsulate who you are, what you do, and what you bring to the table. It's your verbal business card, creating a memorable impression in the limited time of an elevator ride. But networking doesn't end there. Following up after meetings is crucial to solidifying connections. A simple thank-you note or a quick email can warm the relationship, paving the way for future collaborations or opportunities. By showing genuine interest in maintaining contact, you demonstrate professionalism and commitment.

Handling professional criticism with poise is a skill that can set you apart in any workplace. Criticism, when approached constructively, can be a powerful tool for growth. Practice active listening when receiving feedback, focusing on what is being said without jumping to defense. It's essential to understand the underlying intent and reflect on the raised points. Formulating thoughtful responses involves acknowledging the feedback and expressing your willingness to improve rather than reacting impulsively. This approach defuses tension and shows maturity and a commitment to personal development. Constructive engagement with criticism can turn potentially negative experiences into opportunities for learning and growth, enhancing your professional development.

As we conclude this chapter on building conversational confidence, remember that each professional interaction is an opportunity to reflect and grow. You've explored how preparation, nonverbal cues, networking, and handling criticism can enhance your confidence in the workplace. These strategies pave the way for effective communication and build the foundation for successful professional relationships.

CHAPTER 4

ACTIVE LISTENING AND EMPATHY

Imagine you're in a conversation where the person across from you is sharing a story. You nod occasionally and murmur responses, but as they speak, your mind drifts. You're hearing their words, yet not truly grasping the essence of what they're saying. This scenario is all too common, yet it highlights a vital distinction between merely hearing and actively listening. Hearing is a passive act, an automatic response to sound. In contrast, active listening is deliberate and engaged, a cornerstone of effective communication that demands your full attention and empathy. It's about tuning into the speaker's world, as if you are momentarily walking in their shoes, and understanding the meaning behind their words. This approach enriches your conversations and strengthens the bonds you share with others.

At the heart of active listening lies several key components: attention, feedback, and confirmation. Attention involves giving undivided focus to the speaker, free from distractions. This means putting away your phone, making eye contact, and genuinely immersing yourself in the conversation. Feedback is the bridge that connects you and the speaker, showing that you are engaged and present. It can be as simple as a nod or a brief verbal acknowledgment like "I see" or "That makes sense." Confirmation takes it a step further, ensuring mutual understanding by paraphrasing or summarizing the speaker's message. This validates their words and clarifies any potential misunderstandings, creating a shared space of comprehension and respect.

Enhancing your listening skills requires practical strategies that foster deeper engagement. One effective technique is paraphrasing, where you restate what the speaker has said in your own words to confirm understanding. For example, if someone shares their frustration about a work project, you might respond with, "It sounds like you're feeling overwhelmed by the current deadlines." This reflection demonstrates that you not only heard their words but also grasped their emotional context. Additionally, using silence as a tool can be surprisingly powerful. Allowing pauses in conversation gives the speaker room to elaborate and express themselves fully, without feeling rushed or interrupted. This space can lead to richer, more thoughtful exchanges, where both parties feel heard and valued.

However, active listening is not without its challenges. Personal biases can cloud your perception, filtering what you hear through preconceived notions. Being aware of these biases is the first step in managing them. It requires a conscious effort to listen with an open mind, setting aside judgments that might interfere with genuine understanding. Similarly, minimizing distractions is crucial. Whether it's the ping of a new message or the hum of background noise, these interruptions can pull you away from the conversation. Creating an environment conducive to focused listening involves choosing a quiet space, silencing notifications, and being present in the moment. By addressing these obstacles, you pave the way for more meaningful dialogues.

The benefits of active listening are profound, extending across both personal and professional realms. Building trust and credibility is one of the most significant advantages. When people feel truly heard, they are more likely to trust you, forging stronger, more authentic relationships. This trust enhances collaboration, as individuals are more willing to share ideas and work together toward common goals.

Furthermore, active listening bolsters problem-solving capabilities. By understanding different perspectives and gathering comprehensive information, you can approach challenges with greater insight and creativity. These skills are invaluable in any setting, empowering you to navigate complexities with empathy and clarity.

Reflection Section: Practicing Active Listening

Take a moment to reflect on your recent conversations. Were there instances where you felt distracted or misunderstood? Consider practicing active listening in your next interaction by focusing on the speaker and using paraphrasing to ensure understanding. Note the difference in the quality of the conversation and the connection you feel with the other person. This reflection can serve as a guide in honing your active listening skills, leading to more fulfilling interactions.

PRACTICING EMPATHY IN CONVERSATIONS

Empathy, at its core, is about stepping into another person's shoes and seeing the world through their eyes. It's the ability to connect with their emotions, understanding their feelings from their perspective, not just your own. While sympathy might involve feeling sorry for someone else's misfortune, empathy goes deeper, allowing you to experience their emotions alongside them. This distinction is crucial because empathy fosters true connection, while sympathy can sometimes create distance. There are two forms of empathy: cognitive and emotional. Cognitive empathy involves understanding what another person is feeling, while emotional empathy means sharing those feelings. Both are vital in communication, allowing you to respond in ways that are supportive and meaningful.

Developing empathetic skills involves intentional practice and a willingness to engage deeply with others. One effective method is perspective-taking exercises. These involve imagining yourself in the other person's situation, considering how you would feel and what you might think. This mental exercise enhances your ability to connect emotionally and cognitively. Additionally, active listening plays a significant role in developing empathy. By fully attending to what someone is saying, you open yourself up to their emotional experience. This engagement isn't just about hearing words but understanding the context and emotions behind them. Practicing these skills consistently can transform how you interact, making your conversations more meaningful and impactful.

In conflict resolution, empathy serves as a powerful tool for bridging divides and finding common ground. When disagreements arise, acknowledging and validating the other person's feelings can de-escalate tensions and pave the way for productive dialogue. Simple empathy statements like, "I see how this situation is frustrating for you," can diffuse anger and open the door to understanding. By recognizing and expressing empathy, you show a willingness to understand the other person's perspective, which can lead to mutual respect and cooperation. This approach helps in resolving conflicts and strengthens relationships by building a foundation of trust and respect.

The impact of empathy on relationships is profound, influencing how we connect and communicate with those around us. Empathetic communication fosters deeper connections, allowing relationships to flourish. When you express empathy, you signal that you value and understand the other person's experiences, which can strengthen bonds and create lasting connections. Over time, these empathetic interactions build a sense of security and trust, encouraging open and honest communication. Whether in personal or professional settings, empathy enhances collaboration and teamwork, promoting a culture of understanding and mutual support. By practicing empathy consistently, you contribute to a positive environment where everyone feels heard and valued.

Consider the long-term benefits of empathetic communication. In friendships, empathy can deepen your connection, allowing you to support each other through life's challenges. In professional settings, it can enhance teamwork and collaboration, leading to more effective problem-solving and innovation. Examples of empathy in action are all around us —whether it's a manager who listens to an employee's concerns or a friend who offers a shoulder to lean on during tough times. These moments of empathy create ripples, influencing not only the immediate interaction but also the broader dynamics of your relationships. As you cultivate empathy in your interactions, you open the door to richer, more fulfilling connections with those around you.

ECHOING TO BUILD RAPPORT

Imagine you're in a conversation where the other person repeats key phrases you've just used. It might seem simple, but this subtle repetition, known as echoing, is a powerful tool for building rapport and reinforcing connection. Echoing involves reflecting words or phrases, showing that you are truly engaged and present. It tells the other person, "I hear you, and I understand." This technique goes beyond mere words; it acknowledges the speaker's perspective, validating their thoughts and emotions. This subtle mirroring creates a sense of camaraderie, a shared linguistic dance where both parties feel aligned.

Timing and context are crucial when employing echoing effectively. It's not about parroting every word but choosing moments that naturally fit the flow of the conversation. Imagine discussing a project with a colleague, and they mention feeling "overwhelmed by deadlines." By echoing their sentiment—"I can see how those deadlines might feel overwhelming"—you acknowledge their stress and create an opening for further dialogue. This timing makes the speaker feel understood without feeling like you're merely copying them. It's about finding the right moments to weave their language into your response, enhancing the natural rhythm of the conversation.

The benefits of echoing in communication are numerous. When you echo, you reinforce key points, ensuring that the core of the speaker's message is not lost. This reinforcement highlights the importance of their words, showing that you value and respect their input. For instance, in a brainstorming session, echoing a team member's idea—"That's an interesting point about improving customer experience"—can encourage further exploration and discussion. This bolsters the speaker's confidence and fosters an environment where ideas are nurtured and valued. The sense of being heard can transform a simple interaction into a meaningful exchange, building trust and rapport that extend beyond the conversation itself.

However, it's important to strike the right balance. Excessive echoing can come across as insincere or mechanical, undermining the connection you're trying to establish. It's like seasoning a dish; too much can overwhelm the flavor, while just the right amount enhances it. To avoid overuse, focus on the moments where echoing feels genuine and appropriate, where it adds depth to the interaction rather than detracting from it. This balance ensures that your use of echoing remains a natural part of the conversation, enhancing rather than hindering the rapport you seek to build.

As you practice echoing, you'll find that it becomes an intuitive part of your communication style. It fosters an environment of mutual respect and understanding, where both parties feel valued and heard. This technique can transform your interactions, creating connections that are both authentic and lasting. With each conversation, you have the opportunity to build bridges of understanding, one echoed phrase at a time.

RECOGNIZING EMOTIONAL CUES

Imagine you're in a conversation, and the person you're speaking with suddenly changes their tone. They might start with a lively pitch but then shift to a quieter, more subdued voice. These subtle changes can signal a shift in emotion, perhaps indicating discomfort or hesitation. Recognizing these verbal cues is not just about hearing the words; it's about sensing the undercurrents of emotion that accompany them. Similarly, facial expressions and body language are rich with meaning. A furrowed brow, a slight frown, or crossed arms can tell you more than words ever could. These nonverbal signals are like reading a book without text—they add layers of depth to the spoken dialogue, offering insight into what the other person might be feeling. As you become more attuned to these cues, you can respond with greater sensitivity and understanding, creating a more compassionate and empathetic interaction.

Once you identify these emotional cues, responding appropriately becomes crucial. Acknowledging someone's feelings verbally can make a significant difference. Simple statements like, "I can see this is important to you," or "It sounds like you're upset," validate their emotions. This acknowledgment shows that you are not only listening but also deeply attuned to their emotional state. Matching the emotional tone of your response is equally important. If someone is expressing excitement, a lively response from you can keep the energy flowing. Conversely, a calm and measured tone can help soothe anxiety or sadness. This mirroring of emotional tone creates a sense of harmony and understanding, ensuring that your response resonates with the speaker's emotional experience. By doing so, you reinforce the connection and demonstrate genuine empathy.

Improving your ability to recognize these cues involves practice. Role-playing scenarios can be a valuable exercise in honing this skill. By engaging in simulated conversations, you can practice picking up on subtle emotional shifts and responding appropriately. This practice can be done with a friend or even in front of a mirror, allowing you to observe facial expressions and body language closely. Over time, these exercises train your emotional perception, making you more adept at navigating the emotional landscape of real-world interactions. As you refine this skill, you'll find that your communication becomes more nuanced and empathetic, enhancing your ability to connect with others on a meaningful level.

Recognizing and responding to emotional cues significantly impacts the effectiveness of your communication. By tuning into these signals, you enhance mutual understanding and empathy, creating a dialogue that is both authentic and impactful. This heightened awareness builds emotional intelligence, a crucial skill in both personal and professional contexts. When you respond to emotional cues with sensitivity, you foster a supportive environment where open communication thrives. This atmosphere encourages others to share more freely, knowing that their emotions will be met with compassion and respect. The ability to navigate these emotional nuances transforms your interactions, allowing you to engage with others in a way that is both empathetic and empowering.

Developing this skill also contributes to personal growth, as it encourages self-reflection and a deeper understanding of your own emotional responses. As you become more aware of the emotional cues around you, you'll find that your relationships deepen, built on a foundation of trust and empathy. This awareness allows you to engage with others more effectively, creating connections that are not only genuine but also resilient. Recognizing and responding to emotional cues is not just a skill but a way of fostering meaningful relationships that enrich your life.

LISTENING BEYOND WORDS

In the realm of communication, words often take center stage, yet the context surrounding those words can significantly alter their meaning. Understanding this context requires a keen awareness of both cultural and situational factors. Imagine a conversation happening at a bustling market in Japan versus a quiet café in Paris. The cultural norms dictate different communication styles—what might be considered polite in one setting could be perceived as overly formal or even distant in another. Situational context, such as the shared history between speakers or the emotional atmosphere, also plays a crucial role. Without this awareness, you might miss the nuances that give depth to a conversation, leading to misunderstandings or missed connections.

Interpreting unspoken messages requires you to tune into the subtle cues that lie beneath the surface of spoken words. People often communicate more through what they don't say than what they do. Consider the pauses, the hesitations that punctuate a dialogue. A pause might indicate uncertainty, a need for validation, or even a chance for the speaker to gather their thoughts. Reading between the lines involves listening not just to the words, but to the emotions and intentions that accompany them. It's about noticing the shift in energy when a topic is uncomfortable or when enthusiasm suddenly wanes. By being mindful of these unspoken elements, you enhance your ability to respond thoughtfully, strengthening the connection and understanding with the speaker.

Listening for underlying needs and concerns is a skill that goes beyond the surface of what is being said. Often, people's words are a reflection of deeper motivations or fears they might not openly express. Think about a colleague who frequently mentions feeling overwhelmed. While they might be talking about their workload, the underlying need could be for support or understanding. Identifying these motivations requires a blend of empathy and intuition. It's about asking yourself what the speaker might truly need and how you can address those needs in a supportive way. This approach enriches the conversation and fosters a deeper level of trust and rapport.

Applying multilayered listening techniques means engaging with a conversation on multiple levels simultaneously. It's about balancing the content of what is being said with the emotions and intentions behind those words. Reflective listening is a powerful tool in this regard, allowing you to mirror back what you've heard, not just in terms of content but also in capturing the emotional undertones. This technique involves saying something like, "It sounds like you're really passionate about this project," which acknowledges both the words and the emotions conveyed. Such multilayered listening opens the door to deeper insights, uncovering layers of meaning that might otherwise go unnoticed.

In the grand tapestry of communication, listening beyond words is about embracing the full spectrum of human expression. It's about seeing the invisible threads that connect us, the unspoken truths that shape our interactions. By attuning yourself to these subtleties, you transform from a passive listener to an active participant in the conversation. This skill enriches your personal relationships and empowers you in professional settings, where understanding the full context can lead to more effective collaboration and decision-making. As you continue to refine these skills, you'll find that your ability to connect with others deepens, creating pathways for more authentic and meaningful interactions.

As we conclude this chapter, think of listening as not just hearing, but truly understanding beyond words. This skill ties into the broader theme of empathy and connection, paving the way for more genuine interactions. Next, we'll explore how these listening skills enhance digital communication, bridging gaps in our increasingly virtual world.

MAKE A DIFFERENCE
UNLOCK THE POWER OF CONNECTION

"True connection starts with a simple gesture."

— MAYA ANGELOU

Imagine being able to help someone just like you—someone curious about how to communicate better, make friends easily, and feel comfortable talking to anyone. That's the magic of sharing.

With *The Power of How to Talk to Anyone,* my mission is to make connecting with others feel easy and fun for everyone. But to reach more people, I need your help.

Most of us choose books based on what others say about them. By leaving a review, you're helping others find the courage to learn and grow. It's a small act, but it can make a huge difference for someone just beginning their journey.

Your review could help…

- …one more person feel less alone in a crowd.
- …one more student make a new friend.
- …one more worker feel heard and appreciated.
- …one more dream of confidence come true.

Want to make a difference? It costs nothing and takes just a moment. Scan the QR code below to leave a review:

[https://www.amazon.com/review/review-your-purchas
es/?asin=BOOKASIN]

If you're the kind of person who loves helping others, thank
you from the bottom of my heart.

Granite Sparks

CHAPTER 5

DIGITAL COMMUNICATION MASTERY

In today's digital age, your online presence often speaks before you do. Imagine scrolling through your social media feed and seeing profiles that exude authenticity and professionalism, each one a digital handshake. These profiles tell a story that is curated yet genuine, reflecting the person's identity and values. Crafting your digital persona is not just about posting a flattering picture or writing a catchy bio; it's about creating a cohesive narrative across platforms that align with who you are and what you stand for. This chapter delves into the nuances of establishing a digital identity that resonates with your personal and professional aspirations.

Defining your digital identity begins with a consistent visual representation across platforms. Your profile picture is often the first impression people have of you online. It should be professional yet approachable, ideally a high-quality head-shot with a neutral background. This consistency extends to your biography or "about me" section, which should succinctly encapsulate your professional journey and personal ethics. Think of it as your elevator pitch but in digital form. This narrative should be tailored to fit the platform—more formal and detailed on LinkedIn, while allowing for a bit more personality on platforms like Instagram or Twitter. Consistency in visuals and messaging reinforces your brand and builds trust and recognition among your audience.

Adapting your communication style for different digital platforms is essential for maintaining authenticity. Each platform has its own culture and expectations. On LinkedIn, for instance, a professional tone is paramount, focusing on achievements, career goals, and industry insights. Your language should be formal, using industry-specific terminology that highlights your expertise. In contrast, social media platforms like Twitter or Facebook allow for a more conversational tone, where you can infuse your personality and share snippets of your personal life, hobbies, or casual thoughts. This adaptability ensures your communication remains engaging and relevant, allowing your true self to shine through in every post or interaction.

Visual elements play a crucial role in enhancing digital communication, making your content more engaging and memorable. Incorporating infographics into presentations or posts can help distill complex information into easily digestible visuals. These graphics can capture attention, convey data effectively, and enhance understanding. Similarly, using emojis in informal settings adds a layer of emotional expression that text alone might lack. A well-placed emoji can convey a tone, soften criticism, or simply make a message more relatable. However, using them judiciously ensures they complement rather than overshadow your message. Visuals, when used effectively, can amplify your digital presence, making your communication more vibrant and impactful.

Monitoring and evolving your digital persona is an ongoing process. Just as you grow and change, so should your online presence. Regular audits of your social media profiles ensure they accurately reflect your current achievements, interests, and goals. This might involve updating your LinkedIn with new certifications or projects, or refreshing your bio to include recent accomplishments. These updates keep your profiles current and signal to your network that you are actively engaged in your professional development. This adaptability is key to maintaining a dynamic and relevant online presence that resonates with your audience and opens doors to new opportunities.

Reflection Section: Evaluating Your Digital Persona

Take a moment to review your current digital profiles. Consider the following questions: Does your profile picture reflect the image you want to project? Does your biography align with your personal and professional values? Are there any outdated elements that need refreshing? Based on this reflection, jot down a few action items. This exercise will help ensure your digital persona remains authentic and cohesive, ready to engage with your audience effectively.

NAVIGATING EMAIL ETIQUETTE

In the fast-paced world of digital communication, emails remain a cornerstone of professional exchange. Yet, crafting an email that is both clear and effective can be a daunting task. Miscommunication often arises from emails that need to be more concise or clear. A well-structured email begins with clarity and conciseness. Start by organizing your thoughts before you type. Bullet points can be your ally, breaking down information into digestible chunks. They allow readers to grasp the key points quickly without wading through lengthy paragraphs. Equally important is your subject line. It should be a concise summary of the email's content, previewing what lies within. A subject line like "Project Update: Q3 Goals Achieved" immediately informs the reader of the email's purpose, saving them time and setting the right expectation.

Subject lines wield substantial power in the world of email communication. They are the first impression, the hook that captures your recipient's attention amidst a cluttered inbox. A compelling subject line doesn't just inform; it entices. Consider the scenario of sending a follow-up email after a meeting. A subject line such as "Great Meeting Yesterday: Next Steps for Success" reminds the recipient of the meeting and piques interest in the following actions. In contrast, a subject line like "Important Information Inside" might be too vague to generate curiosity or urgency. Tailoring your subject lines to suit the context and audience can significantly impact open rates and engagement, drawing readers into the body of your email.

Balancing formality and friendliness in emails is an art that requires sensitivity to context and audience. An overly casual tone in professional settings might be perceived as disrespectful, while excessive formality can come across as cold or detached. The key lies in striking the right balance. Begin with an appropriate greeting—"Hi [Name]" for a colleague you know well, or "Dear [Title] [Last Name]" for more formal communications. Your closing should mirror this tone, using phrases like "Best regards" or "Warm wishes." This balance extends to the body of your email as well. Use courteous yet approachable language, ensuring your personality shines through without compromising professionalism.

Timely responses in email interactions convey respect and reliability. Picture the frustration of sending an urgent query and waiting days for a reply. It disrupts workflow and creates unnecessary stress. Setting expectations for response times can alleviate this. Let your recipients know when to expect a reply, such as including a note in your signature stating, "I typically respond to emails within 24 hours." This transparency fosters trust and minimizes anxiety. But what about email overload? It's a common challenge, especially in fast-paced environments. Prioritize your inbox by addressing urgent matters first, then schedule specific times in your day to tackle less pressing emails. This approach prevents emails from piling up and ensures you're responsive without feeling overwhelmed.

VIRTUAL MEETING, BEST PRACTICES

Virtual meetings have become a staple of professional life in today's digital landscape. Preparing for these meetings is paramount to ensure they run smoothly and achieve their intended goals. Before your meeting, take the time to test your technology. There's nothing more frustrating than a glitchy connection or malfunctioning microphone when you're trying to make a point. Check your internet connection, test your camera and audio settings, and familiarize yourself with the meeting platform's features. This preparation prevents technical hiccups and sets a professional tone from the outset. Equally important is setting a clear agenda. Share it with participants beforehand so everyone knows what to expect and can prepare accordingly. An agenda acts as a roadmap, guiding the discussion and helping keep the meeting on track and focused.

Engaging participants actively during virtual meetings can be challenging, but it's not impossible. One effective method is to incorporate interactive elements such as polls and Q&A sessions. These tools invite participants to contribute, turning passive listeners into active participants. For instance, a quick survey on a key issue can provide instant feedback and spark a lively discussion. Similarly, dedicating time for a Q&A session allows attendees to voice their thoughts and questions, fostering a collaborative atmosphere. Breakout rooms are another excellent way to encourage engagement. They provide a space for smaller group discussions, enabling more intimate and focused interactions. These rooms can be used for brainstorming sessions or team-building exercises, making the meeting more dynamic and inclusive.

Nonverbal cues may seem less significant in virtual settings but are crucial for conveying engagement and interest. Maintaining eye contact, for instance, is as essential on camera as it is in person. To achieve this, look directly at the camera when speaking rather than at your screen. This minor adjustment makes you appear attentive and engaged, creating a sense of connection with your audience. Use gestures within the camera frame to emphasize points and convey enthusiasm. A nod or hand gesture can emphasize and clarify your message, making your communication more effective. These nonverbal signals help bridge the gap between virtual and face-to-face interactions, ensuring your presence is felt even from afar.

Despite careful preparation, technical difficulties can arise, and handling them with calmness is vital. A backup plan for connectivity issues can help you navigate these challenges smoothly. Consider joining the meeting on a secondary device or keeping a dial-in number handy as a contingency. Communicating effectively during disruptions is equally important. If a technical issue arises, address it promptly and honestly with your participants. Let them know you're aware of the problem and working to resolve it. This transparency reassures attendees and minimizes frustration. Remember, everyone understands that technology can be unpredictable, and how you handle these moments can demonstrate your professionalism and resilience.

TEXTING WITH CLARITY AND WARMTH

Texting has become an integral part of our daily communication, a tool that bridges distances and connects us instantly. Yet, the brevity of texts often leaves room for misinterpretation. Crafting messages that are clear and concise is crucial. Imagine trying to decipher a message filled with jargon or ambiguous language—it can feel like piecing together a puzzle without all the pieces. To avoid this, focus on using straightforward language and punctuation to guide the reader. A simple comma can change the meaning of a sentence, so use them wisely to enhance clarity. For example, "Let's eat, Grandma!" conveys a playful invitation, whereas "Let's eat Grandma!" suggests a rather grim alternative. The difference punctuation makes can be significant, so pay attention to these small details to ensure your message is understood as intended.

Expressing warmth and emotion in text form can seem challenging, but it is achievable with the right tools. Emojis are more than just playful icons; they add a layer of emotional context to your words. A smiley face can convey friendliness, while a heart can express affection. However, use them judiciously to avoid overshadowing your message. Tone indicators, such as "/s" for sarcasm, can also be helpful. They alert the reader to nuances that might be lost in a text. For example, "Wow, you're so early /s" clarifies that the statement is meant sarcastically. These small additions can transform a flat message into one that feels engaging and genuine, bridging the emotional gap that text often creates.

Timing in text communication is another crucial consideration that can impact how your message is received. Imagine receiving a non-urgent text late at night—it might disrupt your peace and inadvertently cause stress. Understanding when to text versus call is vital to respecting others' boundaries. If it's something that can wait, consider timing your messages during reasonable hours unless it's urgent. Observing quiet hours reflects consideration for the recipient's time and privacy. This practice demonstrates respect and builds trust and understanding in your relationships. It's about being mindful of the noise we create in others' lives and choosing to communicate in considerate and thoughtful ways.

Crafting thoughtful responses requires a moment of reflection. It's tempting to fire off a quick reply, but taking a moment to consider your words can make all the difference. Pause before responding to ensure clarity and intent. This not only helps in avoiding misunderstandings but also shows that you value the conversation. Personalizing your messages to reflect your relationship with the recipient adds a personal touch. Let your response echo the familiarity and warmth unique to that connection, whether it's a friend, family member, or colleague. A simple acknowledgment of shared experiences or inside jokes can make your texts feel more intimate and genuine, strengthening your bond.

Interactive Element: Quick Text Check

Before sending your next text, take a moment to ask yourself these questions: Is the message clear and free of ambiguous language? Have you considered the timing and appropriateness of sending it now? Does your response reflect your relationship with the recipient? This quick check ensures your texts are thoughtful and effective, enhancing your digital communication.

BALANCING ONLINE AND OFFLINE INTERACTIONS

In today's digital landscape, relying heavily on virtual connections can be easy, yet blending online and face-to-face interactions offers a richness that neither can achieve alone. Imagine the depth added to your relationships when virtual conversations transition into real-world meetings. Scheduling regular in-person meetups for those you've connected with online can solidify these bonds, transforming a digital acquaintance into a genuine friend. Whether it's a casual coffee with a professional contact or a group gathering with an online community, these face-to-face encounters allow for a level of interaction and understanding that digital communication sometimes lacks. They provide the nuance of shared experiences and the warmth of direct human contact, enriching the connection.

Maintaining authenticity across digital and real-world interactions is crucial in building trust and credibility. Your online persona should be a true reflection of who you are in person. This means aligning your digital presence with your real-world behavior. If you present yourself as approachable and friendly online, ensure this translates into your physical interactions. Consistency in how you engage with others, regardless of the platform, reinforces your authenticity. People appreciate knowing that the person they meet in person is the same as the one they engage with online. This alignment fosters trust and strengthens relationships, making interactions more meaningful and genuine.

Managing digital overload is an ongoing challenge in a world of constant notifications and messages. Setting boundaries for screen time is essential to prevent burnout and maintain a healthy balance. Consider designating specific times for checking emails and social media, allowing for periods of uninterrupted focus on other activities. This practice enhances productivity and ensures digital communication does not infringe on personal time. Additionally, incorporating digital detox techniques into your routine can be beneficial. This might involve taking a weekend without screens or setting aside an hour daily for technology-free activities. These breaks can rejuvenate your mind, reduce stress, and improve your overall well-being, allowing you to return to digital interactions with renewed energy and perspective.

Digital tools can be powerful allies in building and maintaining real-world relationships. Collaborative apps like Trello or Slack can facilitate shared projects, keeping everyone on the same page and enhancing teamwork. They allow for seamless communication and organization, making collaboration more efficient and enjoyable. Additionally, sharing digital calendars for event planning can simplify the process of arranging meetups, ensuring that everyone is informed and engaged. These tools support logistical aspects and enhance the relational dynamics by creating a sense of shared purpose and involvement. By integrating these digital resources, you can strengthen your connections and foster a collaborative environment extending beyond the screen.

As you navigate the intricacies of blending online and offline communication, remember that balance is critical. It's about finding a rhythm that works for you, where digital tools enhance rather than overshadow your real-world interactions. This balance allows you to enjoy the best of both worlds, enriching your relationships with the depth and authenticity they deserve. As we move forward, consider how these principles can be applied to create a sustainable and fulfilling communication practice that supports personal and professional growth.

CHAPTER 6

CULTIVATING CHARISMA AND PRESENCE

I magine stepping into a room where conversation flows like a gentle river and laughter punctuates the air. The energy is magnetic, and you find yourself naturally drawn to specific individuals whose presence commands attention without uttering a word. What makes these people stand out? It's not just their words or their appearance—it's something more profound, an intrinsic quality known as charisma. Contrary to popular belief, charisma isn't an enigmatic trait reserved for the extroverted or the naturally gifted. It's a skill that can be cultivated, a blend of confidence, warmth, and presence that anyone can develop, including you.

Charisma is often described as a magnetic appeal that draws others in, but at its core, it is comprised of three critical elements: confidence, warmth, and presence. Confidence is the belief in your abilities, an assurance that radiates through your demeanor. It's about holding your head high and speaking with conviction. Warmth, on the other hand, is the genuine kindness and empathy you extend to others, creating a welcoming atmosphere. Presence is the ability to fully engage in the moment, making others feel seen and valued. Together, these elements form the foundation of charisma, shaping how you are perceived and how effectively you can connect with others. Authenticity is crucial here—it means being true to yourself while expressing these qualities. When you balance confidence with humility, you create a compelling and relatable persona, inviting others to engage without feeling intimidated.

To cultivate a magnetic energy that naturally draws people in, consider the power of your posture and mindset. A relaxed yet alert posture conveys confidence without arrogance. Stand tall, yet approachable, with open gestures that invite interaction. This body language signals that you are both self-assured and receptive. Positive affirmations can also boost your self-assurance. Start your day by affirming your strengths and potential. Simple statements like "I am confident" or "I am open to connecting with others" can shift your mindset, priming you to engage with the world positively. This inner confidence radiates outward, creating an aura that attracts others.

In group settings, charisma involves more than just standing out; it's about fostering inclusivity and engagement. One effective technique is making eye contact with multiple individuals, ensuring everyone feels included in the conversation. This small gesture creates a sense of connection, signaling that you value each person's presence. Encourage group participation by asking open-ended questions that invite diverse perspectives. For example, instead of asking, "Do you agree?" you might say, "What are your thoughts on this?" This approach enriches the discussion and empowers others to share their insights, creating a dynamic and collaborative environment.

It's essential to differentiate between genuine charisma and manipulation. While both may influence others, the intentions behind them differ significantly. Charisma stems from authenticity and a desire to connect, while manipulation seeks to control or deceive. To maintain genuine charisma, align your actions with your values. Be consistent in your behavior, building trust over time. When your words and actions reflect your true self, you foster relationships built on mutual respect and understanding. This authenticity ensures that your influence is both positive and lasting, creating connections that are meaningful and genuine.

Reflection Section: Cultivating Your Charismatic Presence

Take a moment to reflect on a time when you felt particularly charismatic or connected with others. What elements contributed to this experience? Consider your level of confidence, the warmth you projected, and your presence in the moment. Now, think about how you can apply these elements in future interactions. Write down specific actions you can take to enhance your charisma, such as maintaining eye contact or using open gestures. This reflection will guide you in developing your charismatic presence, allowing you to engage with others more effectively and authentically.

MODULATING YOUR VOCAL TONE

Imagine being in a conversation where the speaker's tone shifts seamlessly, adding layers of meaning and emotion to their words. Herein is the power of vocal tone—a tool that can transform ordinary words into captivating messages. Your tone conveys not just what you say but how you feel about what you're saying. It affects how your message is received, often more than the words themselves. A warm, inviting tone can make others feel at ease, while a sharp, abrupt tone might create a sense of tension. Consider a situation where you're expressing excitement. A lively, energetic tone naturally draws people in, making them eager to share in your enthusiasm. On the other hand, a monotone delivery might dull the impact, leaving your audience disengaged. Recognizing this power allows you to communicate more effectively, tailoring your tone to suit the context and emotion of your message.

Practicing vocal range and dynamics can enrich your communication, adding depth and variety to your speech. Start with diaphragmatic breathing techniques, which involve deep breaths from the diaphragm rather than shallow chest breathing. When using your diaphragm to breathe deeply, your abdomen should extend, and your shoulders should not rise. This method supports your voice and calms your nerves, allowing you to speak with greater control and confidence. Vocal warm-up routines, like those used by singers, can also enhance your range. Simple exercises like humming scales or practicing pitch variations help you explore different tones and volumes. This practice makes your voice more versatile, enabling you to adjust your delivery to suit the mood and message. By expanding your vocal range, you become a more dynamic speaker, capable of engaging and holding your audience's attention.

Using a vocal tone to convey emotion is about matching your voice to the sentiment of your message. When expressing empathy, a soft, gentle tone can communicate understanding and compassion. This subtle shift in your voice can make others feel heard and supported. Conversely, when sharing exciting news, an enthusiastic tone amplifies your words, capturing the listener's attention and drawing them into your excitement. This intentional modulation of tone enhances the emotional impact of your communication, making your interactions more genuine and relatable. You create a connection that goes beyond words, resonating with your audience on a deeper level.

Avoiding monotony in speech is essential for keeping conversations vibrant and engaging. A flat vocal delivery can cause your listeners to lose interest, no matter how compelling your message might be. To counter this, incorporate pauses for emphasis. Strategic pauses give your audience time to absorb your words, adding weight to key points. Varying sentence length and structure also keep your speech dynamic. Short sentences can create urgency, while longer ones allow for detail and nuance. This variation in your delivery prevents boredom and maintains interest, making your communication more impactful and memorable. Please do not overthink this; being natural and expressing your thoughts as they arise will allow you to be genuine.

Exercise: Exploring Your Vocal Dynamics

Try this simple exercise to explore your vocal dynamics: Choose a short passage from a book or article and read it aloud, focusing on varying tone, pitch, and volume. Experiment with different emotions, such as excitement, empathy, and curiosity. Notice how these changes affect the way the passage feels. This practice will help you become more aware of your vocal tone and how to use it to enhance your communication. Repeat the exercise regularly to develop greater control and versatility in your speech.

By embracing the nuances of vocal modulation, you unlock a new dimension of communication. Your voice becomes a powerful tool, conveying a spectrum of emotions and engaging your audience in meaningful ways. When spoken from the heart, your communication can and will evoke emotions from your audience.

STORYTELLING AS A CONVERSATIONAL TOOL

Picture yourself at a dinner table, surrounded by friends or colleagues. The conversation lulls momentarily, and you seize the opportunity to share a story. A well-told tale captivates attention, pulling listeners into a vivid world crafted by your words. The magic of storytelling lies in its structure, composed of a strong hook, a relatable conflict, and a satisfying resolution. The hook is your opening line, designed to capture interest immediately. "Did I ever tell you about when I got lost in a foreign city?" The intrigue is set; your audience leans in, eager to hear more. A compelling conflict follows, perhaps a misunderstanding due to language barriers, creating tension and empathy. The resolution ties everything together, leaving listeners with a lesson, a laugh, a moment of reflection or connection.

Personal anecdotes breathe life into conversations, transforming abstract ideas into tangible experiences. They bridge the gap between you and your audience, making abstract concepts relatable. Choose anecdotes with universal themes such as love, adventure, or growth, as these resonate across diverse backgrounds. For instance, a story about a childhood adventure might evoke fond memories in your listeners, sparking nostalgia and connection. Balance is vital when sharing personal stories. Your tales should be detailed enough to engage but broad enough to remain relevant to the audience. By weaving in your individual experiences, you bring authenticity and depth to your narratives, inviting others to share their stories in return.

Keeping your audience engaged through storytelling involves more than recounting events. It's about painting a picture with your words, using sensory details to create vivid imagery. Describe the aroma of fresh pastries wafting through the air or the vibrant colors of a bustling market. These details transport listeners, immersing them in the narrative. Engage the senses to make your stories come alive, allowing your audience to feel, see, and hear the world you're describing. Encourage participation by inviting feedback or questions. Ask, "What would you have done in my situation?" This invitation transforms passive listeners into active participants, fostering a dynamic exchange that deepens the connection.

Adapting stories to different contexts ensures that your message resonates with various audiences. The same story can take on new life depending on the setting and the people involved. Adjust the complexity of your language based on the familiarity of your listeners. A casual tone and insider jokes might be appropriate for a group of close friends. A more formal approach with relevant industry insights would be better suited in a professional setting. Align your stories with cultural norms to avoid misunderstandings and ensure inclusivity. Understanding your audience's background and preferences allows you to tailor your stories effectively, creating a shared experience that resonates deeply.

Interactive Element: Crafting Your Story

Think of a personal experience that taught you a valuable lesson or left a lasting impression. Break it down into the three key elements: hook, conflict, and resolution. Write a draft focusing on sensory details and emotional impact. Share it with a friend or colleague and ask for their feedback on clarity and engagement. This exercise will help refine your storytelling skills, ensuring your narratives are captivating and meaningful.

As you develop your storytelling abilities, remember that stories are more than entertainment. They are bridges that connect us, allowing us to share our experiences and learn from each other. They create moments of empathy and understanding, drawing listeners into a shared human experience. Embrace the power of storytelling to enrich your conversations, transforming them into memorable and impactful interactions.

CREATING MEMORABLE IMPRESSIONS

What comes to mind when you think about someone who leaves a lasting impression? It's often a blend of uniqueness, authenticity, and emotional engagement. These are the elements that make an encounter memorable. Uniqueness can be your personal style or a signature element that sets you apart. It might be how you wear a particular piece of clothing or the distinctiveness of your laugh. Authenticity means being true to yourself and allowing your genuine personality to shine through. When people feel they are seeing the real you, it fosters a connection that remains beyond the initial meeting. Emotional impact is about how you make others feel. Did you evoke joy, comfort, or inspiration? These feelings linger, creating a memory that sticks. Consistency in your messaging and appearance reinforces this impression. When your words and actions align, you project reliability and trustworthiness, further solidifying the impression you make.

In professional settings, first impressions hold significant weight. It is often said that people form an opinion within the first few seconds of meeting someone. To make these moments count, consider crafting a personal introduction that is both concise and impactful. Think about what you want others to remember about you. A clear and compelling introduction can set the tone for the rest of your interaction. In addition to your words, your appearance speaks volumes. Dressing appropriately for the occasion conveys respect and professionalism. It indicates that you are serious about the encounter and value the opportunity to connect. This combination of a strong introduction and appropriate attire creates a powerful first impression that can open doors and pave the way for professional relationships.

Leaving a lasting emotional impact involves engaging with others on a deeper level. When used appropriately, humor can be a fantastic tool to lighten the mood. A well-timed joke or light-hearted comment can ease tension and create a sense of camaraderie. However, it is beneficial to be mindful of the context and ensure that your humor is inclusive and respectful. Demonstrating genuine interest in others' stories also leaves a positive mark. People appreciate when you take the time to listen and engage with what they have to say. Ask thoughtful questions, and show empathy and understanding. These interactions make people feel valued and respected, leaving them with a positive impression that endures.

Consistency is valuable in reinforcing the impressions you make. You create a cohesive and authentic presence when your verbal messages align with your nonverbal cues. For example, if you express enthusiasm about a project, ensure that your body language reflects this excitement. Your gestures, facial expressions, and tone of voice should all support your words. This alignment reinforces your message and makes it more believable. Following up on initial encounters is another way to maintain consistency. If you promised to send information or connect someone with a contact, make sure you follow through. These actions demonstrate reliability and integrity, reinforcing your initial positive impression.

Creating memorable impressions is about more than just the initial encounter. It's the ongoing interactions that solidify how others perceive you. Consider each interaction an opportunity to reinforce the image you want to project. Whether meeting someone for the first time or nurturing an existing relationship, the principles of uniqueness, authenticity, and emotional engagement remain the same. These elements are the building blocks of memorable impressions that resonate long after the conversation ends.

DEVELOPING A CAPTIVATING PRESENCE

Your presence is the unique energy you bring into a room, the blend of personality and poise that commands attention and respect. Developing a captivating presence begins with cultivating a strong personal brand that reflects your values and aspirations personally and professionally. This brand is not about creating a façade but highlighting the authentic qualities that define you. Consider what attributes you want to be known for—integrity, creativity, empathy, resilience—and let these guide your interactions and decisions. Craft a personal branding statement that encapsulates these traits, serving as a compass for your actions and communications.

This statement should be clear and concise, a reflection of both your current identity and the person you aspire to become. You create a coherent presence that others can easily recognize and trust by consistently aligning your actions with your personal brand.

Body language is a silent yet powerful tool in shaping how others perceive you. It contributes significantly to your presence, often speaking louder than words. A confident stance, with shoulders back and head held high, projects assurance and openness. This posture invites others to engage, signaling that you are approachable and engaged. Gestures play a crucial role as well. Open palms and relaxed movements suggest honesty and a willingness to connect, while crossed arms or fidgeting might convey discomfort or defensiveness. By being mindful of your body language, you can ensure that it complements your verbal communication, creating a harmonious and captivating presence. Practice these techniques regularly so they become second nature, enhancing your ability to connect with others authentically and effectively.

Radiating confidence and calmness is essential, especially in stressful situations. These traits help you maintain composure and reassure those around you. Mindfulness practices, such as deep breathing and meditation, are valuable tools for cultivating inner peace. They allow you to center yourself, finding calm amidst the chaos. Visualization techniques can also boost self-assurance. Picture yourself successfully navigating a challenging interaction, engaging with poise and clarity. This mental rehearsal reinforces your confidence, preparing you to face real-world situations easily. By embracing these practices, you project an aura of calm and control, encouraging others to feel comfortable and confident in your presence.

Adapting your presence to suit different environments is a skill that enhances your impact and relevance. A more reserved demeanor may be appropriate in formal settings, focusing on professionalism and clarity. Meanwhile, informal gatherings call for a relaxed and approachable attitude. Modulating your presence involves reading the room, observing the energy and dynamics, and adjusting your behavior accordingly. This adaptability ensures that your presence resonates with the context, allowing you to connect with diverse audiences without compromising authenticity.

By developing this flexibility, you become more adept at navigating various social landscapes and creating meaningful connections across different settings.

As you refine your ability to develop a captivating presence, remember that it's the blend of authenticity, adaptability, and awareness that truly makes you stand out. These skills enrich your interactions and enhance your professional endeavors, opening doors to new opportunities and connections. With a solid personal brand, mindful body language, and the ability to adapt to different environments, you create a presence that is both memorable and impactful.

CHAPTER 7

HANDLING DIFFICULT CONVERSATIONS

Picture this: you're at work, and the tension is so thick you could cut it with a knife. It's a meeting where emotions simmer just below the surface, ready to boil over at any moment. Everyone's eyes darted around the room as if searching for an escape route. We've all been there, caught in the web of a difficult conversation where words can feel like weapons and silence can be deafening. But what if these interactions didn't have to feel so daunting? What if we approached them with poise and preparedness instead of dread?

Understanding the roots of conflict is essential in untangling these challenging dialogues. Often, disagreements arise not from the apparent issue at hand but from deeper, unaddressed concerns. Imagine a conflict where the surface argument is about missing deadlines, but underneath, it's fueled by feelings of being undervalued. Grasping this distinction is paramount. It's about peeling away the layers of the conversation to reveal the deeper issues at play. On the surface, a disagreement might appear to be about one topic, like missed deadlines, but probing deeper can unveil a more complex web of emotions and unmet needs, such as feeling undervalued or overlooked. This understanding shifts the focus of your approach. It's not merely about resolving the immediate disagreement but addressing the root cause that fuels the fire. Doing so will pave the way for a more meaningful resolution and foster a deeper connection and understanding between all parties involved. It allows you to address the real problem rather than merely skimming the surface. Emotional triggers are often at the heart of conflicts, causing reactions that may seem disproportionate to the situation. Identifying these triggers can transform your approach, making you more empathetic and persuasive. By acknowledging the underlying feelings—whether it be insecurity, fear, or frustration—you can navigate conversations with a clearer understanding of the emotional landscape.

Adopting a calm and open mindset is a powerful tool in your conflict-resolution arsenal. It starts with a simple yet profound act: breathing. Deep, mindful breaths can anchor you, slowing your heart rate and clearing your mind. Before engaging in a difficult conversation, take a moment to breathe deeply, focusing on the inhale and exhale. Take a deep breath in through your nose, letting your abdomen expand, and then exhale slowly out of your mouth. Count to 4 and then repeat the breathing exercise a few times, focusing on the silence underlying any noise surrounding you. This practice grounds you, reduces anxiety and prepares you for the discussion ahead. Set a clear intention for the conversation, aiming for a constructive outcome. This intention acts as your guiding star, keeping the dialogue on course even when emotions threaten to steer it off track. Approaching the conversation with openness means being willing to listen and adapt, creating space for a genuine exchange of ideas.

Setting the stage for productive dialogue involves creating an environment where communication can thrive. Choose a neutral location for your conversation, a space that doesn't hold the weight of previous conflicts or power dynamics. This neutrality can foster openness, making it easier for both parties to engage without feeling defensive. Establish ground rules for the discussion, emphasizing respect and active listening. These rules act as a framework, guiding the conversation and ensuring it remains productive and civil. Setting these expectations upfront creates a safe space where honesty and vulnerability are met with understanding rather than judgment.

The language you use can either bridge gaps or widen them. Opt for language that promotes understanding and collaboration. "I" statements are a cornerstone of effective communication. They allow you to express your feelings and needs without casting blame. Instead of saying, "You're always interrupting me," try, "I feel unheard when I'm interrupted." This subtle shift in language can diffuse defensiveness, paving the way for a more open and constructive dialogue. Avoid blame-laden language that can escalate tension and derail the conversation. Focus on expressing your perspective and inviting the other person to share theirs. This approach fosters collaboration and builds trust, allowing you to work together toward a resolution.

Reflection Section: Reframing Conflict

Consider a recent conflict you experienced. Reflect on the underlying issues that may have contributed to the disagreement. What emotional triggers were at play, and how did they influence the conversation? Write down your observations and think about how a calm and open mindset and constructive language might have altered the outcome. Use this reflection to inform your approach in future conversations, allowing you to navigate conflict with greater empathy and understanding.

As you navigate difficult conversations, remember that each interaction is an opportunity for growth. By understanding the roots of conflict, adopting a calm and open mindset, setting the stage for productive dialogue, and using language that promotes understanding, you transform these challenges into opportunities for connection and resolution.

TECHNIQUES FOR DE-ESCALATING TENSION

Navigating the stormy seas of a heated conversation requires a keen awareness of the subtle signs that tension is rising. You might notice voices climbing to louder volumes as if each word attempts to make one's position known over the clamor of emotions. Body language becomes a symphony of crossed arms and tense postures, signals that defensiveness is setting in. Interruptions pierce the flow of dialogue like sudden gusts of wind, each one a dismissive gesture that fans the flames of conflict. Recognizing these signs is not just about observing others; it's about tuning into the energy of the room and understanding when a conversation teeters on the edge of escalation. By staying attuned to these cues, you become better equipped to intervene before the situation spirals out of control.

Once you've recognized the signs, applying de-escalation techniques becomes your lifeline to restoring calm. Sometimes, the most powerful action is inaction—a deliberate pause that allows heated emotions to cool. Simply suggesting a break can give both parties the space to breathe and reflect, creating a buffer between reaction and response. Humor can also be a powerful tool, a gentle breeze that disperses tension. When used appropriately, a lighthearted comment or shared laugh can break the cycle of anger, reminding everyone involved of their shared humanity. However, humor must be wielded with care, ensuring it doesn't come across as dismissive or out of touch with the gravity of the situation. By pausing the conversation and introducing levity, you redirect the focus, opening the door to resolution. It may also pay dividends to suggest ending there and resuming the conversation at a point where emotions are not so elevated in the near future. Searching for a win-win situation can help to de-escalate the situation and create the understanding that you are interested in making things work to the benefit of both parties.

Focusing on common goals serves as the compass that guides a conversation back on course. In the heat of conflict, it's easy to become entrenched in opposing positions, losing sight of the shared objectives that unite you. Reframing the issues at hand to emphasize mutual benefits can transform adversaries into allies. Consider the overlapping interests that brought you together in the first place, whether it's a shared project at work or a mutual desire for a harmonious home life. Highlighting these commonalities reminds everyone involved of the larger picture, shifting the narrative from "me versus you" to "us." You may then bridge divides by identifying these shared values and goals, fostering collaboration and understanding.

Acknowledging and validating emotions is the linchpin in reducing defensiveness and promoting open dialogue. When someone feels heard, they're more likely to lower their defenses and engage constructively. Reflecting back on the emotions you perceive, such as saying, "It sounds like you're very frustrated by this situation," shows that you understand their perspective. This simple act of acknowledgment can deflate tension, signaling that you are listening and empathizing. Offering empathetic statements, like "I can see this is important to you," reinforces that their feelings are valid and that you're committed to addressing their concerns. This validation creates a safe space where honest communication can flourish, paving the way for resolution.

Interactive Element: De-escalation Practice

Consider a recent conversation that escalated. Reflect on the signs you noticed and which de-escalation techniques you might have used. Write down a plan for how you could approach a similar situation differently in the future, focusing on recognizing escalation signs, applying calming techniques, and uniting over shared goals. Use these reflections as a guide to practice in future interactions, transforming conflict into an opportunity for growth and understanding.

As you integrate these techniques into your conversations, you'll find that the tools of de-escalation are about calming stormy seas and steering toward calmer waters. Recognizing signs of escalation, applying strategic pauses and humor, focusing on shared objectives, and validating emotions are all steps toward healthier, more constructive dialogues.

CONSTRUCTIVE FEEDBACK FRAMEWORKS

Embarking on a feedback session can often feel like navigating a minefield, yet with careful preparation, it can transform into an opportunity for growth and understanding. The first step in preparing for effective feedback is setting a clear agenda, knowing precisely what you want to discuss and why it matters. Clarity reduces ambiguity, allowing both parties to focus on the points that truly need attention. Choose an appropriate time and setting for the conversation—somewhere private and comfortable, away from the distractions and pressures of the everyday hustle. Timing is crucial; you want the recipient to be receptive and not preoccupied with other tasks. By scheduling feedback during a calm moment, you set the tone for a constructive conversation rather than an argumentative one.

Once you've prepared, structured feedback models can provide a roadmap for clearly delivering your message. The Situation-Behavior-Impact (SBI) framework is particularly effective. This model encourages you to describe the specific situation, the observed behavior, and its impact on the team or project. For instance, instead of saying, "You're always late," you might say, "During yesterday's team meeting, when you arrived late, it disrupted the flow of our discussion and delayed our decisions." This approach removes personal attacks and focuses on observable actions and their consequences, making it easier for the recipient to understand and accept the feedback. It shifts the focus from blame to behavior, encouraging reflection and change. You highlight why the behavior matters by clearly outlining the impact and making the feedback relevant and actionable.

Feedback should never be a one-way street. It thrives on being a dialogue, not a monologue. Encouraging a two-way conversation fosters engagement and mutual understanding. Invite the recipient to share their perspective. Ask open-ended questions like, "How do you feel about this feedback?" or "What do you think might help address this issue?" These questions show respect for the recipient's viewpoint and open the floor for collaborative problem-solving. It's about creating a space where both parties feel heard, leading to a more balanced and enriching exchange. This collaborative approach can uncover insights you might have overlooked and lead to innovative solutions that benefit everyone involved.

Following up on feedback is the key to ensuring that the conversation leads to tangible change. After the initial discussion, schedule follow-up meetings to assess progress and discuss any challenges the recipient may face. This continued engagement demonstrates your commitment to their development and reinforces the importance of the feedback. Encourage self-reflection and goal-setting during these follow-ups, helping the recipient to take ownership of their growth. By setting specific, achievable goals, they can track their progress and celebrate their successes along the way. This ongoing dialogue keeps the feedback relevant, transforming it from a momentary critique into a sustained journey of improvement and learning.

MAINTAINING COMPOSURE UNDER PRESSURE

Maintaining your composure in the heat of a high-pressure conversation can feel like walking a tightrope. Emotions swirl and the stakes often seem sky-high. However, regulating your emotions is crucial for handling these tense moments with poise. One effective technique is practicing mindfulness and meditation. These practices encourage you to focus on the present, helping to calm the mind and body. Mindfulness involves observing your thoughts and feelings without judgment, creating a sense of inner peace even when external situations are challenging.

Conversely, meditation can deepen this sense of calm, allowing you to approach conversations with a centered and balanced mindset. Grounding techniques, such as focusing on your breath or feeling your feet firmly on the ground, can also help you stay present. These simple but powerful practices anchor you, reducing reactivity and enhancing your ability to respond thoughtfully.

Building a resilient mindset is another fundamental strategy for maintaining composure. Resilience is like a mental muscle strengthened through experience and reflection. By focusing on long-term goals rather than short-term discomfort, you can keep your perspective in check. This shift in focus helps you view complex interactions as temporary hurdles rather than insurmountable obstacles. Reflecting on past experiences—where you faced challenges and emerged stronger—can bolster your resolve. No matter how tough, each interaction contributes to your growth and builds your capacity to handle future challenges with greater ease. Embracing resilience means accepting that setbacks are part of the process and that perseverance is your ally.

Assertiveness is vital to effective communication, particularly when expressing your needs and boundaries. It's about speaking up for yourself confidently and clearly without veering into aggression. When someone makes a request that you can't accommodate, practice declining firmly yet politely. Phrases like "I'm unable to take that on right now" or "I need to prioritize other commitments" convey your boundaries without alienating the other person. Assertive body language—such as maintaining a firm posture and steady eye contact—reinforces your words, signaling that you mean what you say. This combination of verbal and nonverbal cues creates a powerful message that you are respectful and committed.

Recognizing your limits is crucial in maintaining composure and preventing burnout. It's easy to overextend yourself, especially when you're eager to please or prove your worth. But knowing when to set boundaries is essential for your well-being. Clearly define the limits of your engagement, whether it's the number of projects you can handle or the time you need for rest and rejuvenation. This self-awareness allows you to allocate your energy effectively, ensuring you can remain composed despite high demands. Don't hesitate to step back or seek assistance when needed. Asking for help is not a sign of weakness; it's a strategic move that preserves your strength and enables you to contribute more effectively in the long run. Recognizing when to pause and recharge ensures you can approach each conversation with the calm and focus it deserves.

EMPATHY IN CONFLICT RESOLUTION

In the heat of conflict, emotions can cloud judgment, making seeing all sides of an issue challenging. This is where empathy becomes a powerful ally. Empathy allows you to step into the other person's shoes, seeing the world from their perspective. It requires active listening, not just hearing words but truly absorbing the emotions and context behind them. When someone expresses frustration, pause and consider their feelings instead of immediately countering with your viewpoint. What might they be experiencing that leads them to feel this way? Engage in perspective-taking exercises by imagining how you might react in their situation. This deliberate shift in focus can illuminate shared human experiences, fostering a connection that transcends disagreement. By embracing empathy, you open the door to a deeper understanding, which is often the first step toward resolving conflict.

Demonstrating empathy can be a bridge to trust, an essential component of conflict resolution. Trust is built when people feel their emotions and concerns are acknowledged. Sharing your own experiences can be a powerful way to show understanding. Say you're discussing a challenging project deadline; mentioning a time when you faced similar pressures can create a bond of shared experience. It tells the other person that their feelings are valid and that they're not alone. Simply acknowledging their emotions—saying, "I can see why this is upsetting"—can go a long way. It indicates that you're not dismissing their concerns but rather honoring them. This validation is crucial in breaking down barriers, making it easier to navigate the path to resolution together.

Language plays a crucial role in conveying empathy and understanding. The words you choose can either build bridges or erect walls. Phrases like "I understand where you're coming from" demonstrate that you've taken the time to consider their perspective. This kind of language opens up a channel for dialogue, encouraging openness and honesty. It tells the other person that you're not just listening to respond but listening to understand. Such empathetic language can transform a combative atmosphere into one of collaboration, where both parties feel valued and heard. It's a subtle yet powerful tool that can shift the entire dynamic of a conversation.

While empathy is vital, it must be balanced with objectivity, especially in conflict situations. Empathy should never cloud your judgment or lead you to overlook important facts. Evaluating the situation objectively means considering all aspects, including emotions and tangible evidence. This balance ensures that decisions are fair and well-rounded. It's about acknowledging feelings without letting them override the reality of the situation. In doing so, you maintain integrity and fairness, creating solutions that respect both emotional and factual elements. This dual approach fosters an environment where empathy and rationality coexist, guiding you toward resolutions that are both compassionate and equally equitable.

As we wrap up this chapter, it's clear that handling difficult conversations with empathy is about more than just resolving conflict. It's about building relationships that can withstand challenges, grounded in trust and understanding. With these tools, you're better equipped to transform conflict into opportunities for growth and connection. As we move forward, we'll explore how these principles can be applied to build rapport across diverse cultures, further enriching your communication skills.

CHAPTER 8

BUILDING RAPPORT ACROSS CULTURES

You're in a bustling marketplace in a foreign land, surrounded by a symphony of unfamiliar sounds and sights. You're eager to connect and engage with the local culture but hesitate, uncertain of the nuances that dictate these interactions. It's a common scenario that plays out in varying forms across our increasingly globalized world. Establishing rapport across cultures can feel like navigating a labyrinth, where every turn presents new challenges and opportunities for connection. Yet, the potential for profound understanding and enriched relationships lies in this complex web of diverse customs and languages. By delving into cultural nuances, you can transform these encounters into rewarding experiences.

Understanding cultural differences begins with recognizing the fundamental norms and practices that vary from one culture to another. Anthropologist Edward T. Hall introduced the concept of high-context and low-context cultures, shedding light on how different societies communicate. Much of the communication in high-context cultures like Japan and Brazil relies on implicit understanding, shared experiences, and nonverbal cues. Here, a nod or a pause can carry as much weight as spoken words. Conversely, low-context cultures like the United States and Australia emphasize explicit, direct communication, where words are the primary conveyors of meaning. Recognizing where a culture falls on this spectrum can help you tailor your communication approach, ensuring clarity and respect. For example, attention to the subtleties of body language and tone is essential in high-context settings. At the same time, in low-context environments, clear and concise verbal exchanges are valued.

Hierarchy and authority also play significant roles in shaping cultural interactions. In some cultures, respect for authority and age is deeply ingrained, influencing how people address each other and make decisions. For instance, in many Asian cultures, seniority is highly respected, and deference to elders is common. In these settings, understanding the appropriate level of formality and knowing when to seek input from those in higher positions can be crucial. In contrast, cultures that value egalitarianism, such as those in Scandinavia, tend to emphasize equality and encourage open dialogue across all levels. Being mindful of these differences helps you navigate social and professional interactions with grace and sensitivity, fostering mutual respect and understanding.

Respecting cultural traditions and practices is paramount when building rapport. This respect can manifest in various ways, from observing appropriate greetings and gestures to acknowledging significant cultural holidays and events. In some cultures, a handshake might be the norm, while a bow or a nod is more appropriate in others. Familiarizing yourself with these customs shows that you value and honor the culture, paving the way for meaningful connections. Additionally, recognizing and celebrating cultural events can further deepen your understanding. For example, participating in or acknowledging festivals and holidays enriches your cultural experience and demonstrates genuine interest and respect for the traditions that hold significance to those you engage with.

Learning from cultural guides and resources can help you gain deeper insights into specific cultures. Books and articles on cultural etiquette provide valuable knowledge about different customs and communication styles. Engaging with cultural consultants or attending workshops can offer hands-on experience and personalized guidance. These resources equip you with the tools needed to approach multicultural interactions with confidence and awareness. Investing time in understanding the nuances of different cultures enhances your ability to connect authentically and effectively.

Developing cultural intelligence is a skill that enables you to navigate multicultural interactions with ease and adaptability. It involves observing and adapting your behavior based on cultural cues and practicing open-mindedness and flexibility in unfamiliar settings. Cultural intelligence goes beyond knowledge; it's about applying that knowledge in real-world scenarios. By remaining receptive to new experiences and perspectives, you cultivate an environment where diverse voices are heard and valued. This adaptability enriches your personal and professional relationships and creates a foundation for collaboration and innovation.

Reflection Section: Exploring Cultural Nuances

Reflect on a recent interaction where cultural differences played a role. Consider how the communication style, hierarchy, or traditions influenced the exchange. What did you learn, and how did you adapt your approach? Take a moment to journal your thoughts, noting any insights or areas for growth. Use this reflection to guide future interactions, striving to build bridges across cultural divides.

ADAPTING COMMUNICATION FOR INCLUSIVITY

Imagine you're sitting in a meeting with colleagues from around the globe. Each person brings a unique perspective shaped by their cultural background and experiences. As you begin to communicate, the importance of tailoring your language and tone becomes evident. Using simple, straightforward language helps bridge cultural divides, reducing the risk of misunderstandings. Complex idioms or jargon, often rooted in specific cultural contexts, can create barriers. For instance, a phrase like "the ball is in your court" might puzzle someone unfamiliar with its symbolic meaning. Instead, opting for straightforward language ensures that everyone can engage fully in the conversation regardless of their cultural background.

Language barriers are a common challenge in multicultural settings but are not insurmountable. Embracing tools and strategies to overcome these barriers can transform potential obstacles into opportunities for connection. Translation tools and services are invaluable resources, allowing for real-time communication despite language differences. These tools can facilitate smoother interactions, ensuring that messages are conveyed accurately. Additionally, learning basic phrases in another language demonstrates respect and effort, even if fluency is yet to be achieved. A simple "thank you" or "hello" in someone's native tongue can go a long way in building rapport and showing genuine interest in their culture.

Encouraging diverse perspectives enriches conversations and fosters an inclusive environment. When people from varied backgrounds share their insights, it broadens the scope of understanding and opens up new possibilities. Creating opportunities for all voices to be heard involves actively inviting input from everyone, especially those who hesitate to speak up. It requires recognizing and challenging personal biases that may influence whose opinions are valued. By consciously making space for diverse contributions, you cultivate a culture of inclusivity where every perspective is respected and considered. This approach enhances individual interactions and strengthens team dynamics, driving innovation and creativity.

Promoting inclusive dialogue involves establishing norms that ensure everyone feels comfortable sharing their thoughts and ideas. Setting ground rules for respectful conversation creates a safe space where individuals can express themselves without fear of judgment or exclusion. These norms include practices such as active listening, where you focus entirely on the speaker without interrupting and using inclusive language that embraces diversity. Inclusive language goes beyond words; it reflects attitudes and values, prioritizing empathy and respect. Choosing words that acknowledge and celebrate differences lays the foundation for meaningful exchanges that transcend cultural boundaries.

When engaging with diverse groups, remaining open to learning and adapting is essential. Flexibility and curiosity drive successful cross-cultural communication. As you interact with individuals from different backgrounds, be prepared to adjust your communication style based on the context and the preferences of those you're engaging with. This adaptability demonstrates a willingness to learn and grow, fostering mutual respect and understanding. It also encourages others to reciprocate, creating a dynamic where everyone is both a teacher and a student. In this way, communication becomes a shared journey of discovery, where cultural differences are not obstacles but enrichment opportunities.

In your interactions, remember that inclusivity is not just about accommodating differences; it's about celebrating them. Each culture brings its own unique strengths and perspectives, enriching the tapestry of human experience. By embracing these differences, you enhance your communication skills and contribute to a more interconnected and harmonious world. Whether in personal relationships or professional collaborations, the ability to adapt communication for inclusivity opens doors to deeper understanding and lasting connections. This approach enriches your experience and empowers those around you to engage more fully and authentically.

AVOIDING CULTURAL PITFALLS

Imagine walking into a room filled with people from diverse cultures, each with unique stories and backgrounds. You're eager to connect, yet you find yourself hesitant, aware of the weight that stereotypes can carry. They are like invisible walls that confine our understanding, reducing multifaceted individuals to simplistic caricatures. For instance, assuming that all Germans are punctual or that all Italians gesticulate wildly limits your perspective and hinders genuine connections. Stereotypes, often born from limited exposure or media portrayal, fail to capture the complexity of cultural identities. They can create barriers of misunderstanding, leading to superficial and strained interactions. Recognizing the dangers of stereotypes is the first step in dismantling them, allowing you to approach each person as an individual, unencumbered by preconceived notions. Doing so opens the door to authentic interactions that celebrate diversity rather than diminish it.

Cultural sensitivities are the unspoken nuances that color our interactions. They vary widely, often touching on deeply personal or societal values. Topics such as politics, religion, and personal relationships can be delicate areas where a misstep might cause discomfort or offense. In some cultures, discussing politics is as common as discussing the weather; in others, it is considered highly sensitive. Understanding these sensitivities requires more than just knowledge; it demands empathy and awareness. It means listening actively, observing reactions, and adjusting your approach to respect the boundaries of those you engage with. Doing so demonstrates cultural competence and a genuine respect for the person behind the culture.

Navigating taboos and sensitive topics involves a careful balance of curiosity and respect. Certain gestures or phrases, perfectly acceptable in one culture, may be considered rude or inappropriate in another. For example, the thumbs-up gesture, common in Western cultures, can be offensive in parts of the Middle East. Awareness of these subtleties allows you to engage with others thoughtfully, avoiding pitfalls that might inadvertently harm relationships. When encountering sensitive topics, approach them with a spirit of inquiry rather than assumption. Ask open-ended questions and be willing to learn from the responses you receive. This approach enriches your understanding and fosters an environment of mutual respect and openness.

To enhance your cultural sensitivity, actively seek feedback from those around you. Colleagues or friends from different cultural backgrounds can offer valuable insights into your interactions, highlighting areas where you might inadvertently perpetuate stereotypes or overlook sensitivities. Encourage honest dialogue, where feedback is seen as a gift rather than a critique. Reflecting on past interactions with an open mind can reveal patterns and areas for improvement. Consider what went well and what might have been handled differently. This reflective practice helps you cultivate a mindset of continuous learning and adaptation, allowing you to grow in your cultural understanding and empathy.

By engaging with others in this way, you demonstrate a commitment to building bridges across cultural divides. It's not about achieving perfection but about striving for connection and understanding. Each interaction becomes an opportunity to learn, listen, and expand your horizons. As you navigate the rich tapestry of cultural diversity, you enhance your communication skills and contribute to a world where differences are celebrated and embraced. Each step you take towards understanding and respect brings you closer to the heart of authentic human connection.

BUILDING BRIDGES IN MULTICULTURAL SETTINGS

You're sitting in a room filled with people from around the world, each bringing their own stories and backgrounds. There's a palpable energy, a sense of potential waiting to be unlocked. In such moments, fostering mutual respect and understanding becomes the cornerstone of building lasting bridges. It's about seeing beyond the surface and celebrating the rich tapestry of cultural diversity that each individual brings. Shared experiences—whether through stories, traditions, or even food—can serve as powerful connectors. Imagine sharing a meal that blends Indian spices with Italian pasta, each ingredient a nod to the cultures represented at the table. These shared moments create a foundation for mutual respect, where differences are acknowledged and embraced. They remind us that while our backgrounds may vary, our shared humanity binds us together.

Cross-cultural collaborations offer a fertile ground for strengthening relationships and honing skills. By joining multicultural teams or participating in projects that span various cultural backgrounds, you open yourself up to a wealth of perspectives and expertise. These collaborations are not merely about completing tasks; they are about learning from one another, challenging preconceived notions, and growing together. Consider the benefits of participating in cultural exchange programs, where immersion in another culture offers firsthand insights into different ways of thinking and problem-solving. These experiences broaden your worldview, equipping you with the adaptability and empathy needed to thrive in diverse environments. As you engage with others, you learn to appreciate the similarities and differences that make each culture unique.

Leveraging cultural strengths is a powerful strategy for enhancing creativity and innovation. Each culture brings unique problem-solving approaches shaped by historical context, societal values, and environmental factors. In Japan, for instance, the concept of "kaizen" emphasizes continuous improvement through small, incremental changes. This approach has been widely adopted in business settings, fostering a culture of innovation and adaptability. By recognizing and highlighting these diverse problem-solving methods, you can harness the collective strengths of a multicultural team. Encouraging creativity through cultural diversity means valuing each individual's contributions and creating an environment where new ideas are welcomed and nurtured. This inclusive approach fosters a sense of belonging, where everyone feels empowered to contribute their best.

Creating a culture of inclusion goes beyond mere representation; it involves actively valuing diversity as an asset. Implementing diversity and inclusion initiatives within organizations sets the stage for a more equitable and harmonious environment. These initiatives might include mentorship programs, diversity training, or community-building activities emphasizing collaboration and mutual respect. By recognizing and rewarding inclusive behavior, you reinforce the importance of diversity as a driving force for innovation and growth. It's about creating a space where every voice is heard and valued, where differences are seen as strengths rather than obstacles. This inclusive culture enhances individual well-being and contributes to a more dynamic and resilient organization capable of navigating the complexities of a globalized world.

As you continue to explore these themes, consider how building bridges across cultures enriches your life and those around you. Each interaction is an opportunity to learn, grow, and connect on a deeper level. In embracing diversity, you enhance your communication skills and contribute to a world where understanding and respect transcend borders. These bridges we build are not just for today but for future generations, laying the groundwork for a more inclusive and interconnected world. As we transition into the next chapter, keep in mind the power of these connections and the potential they hold for creating meaningful change.

CHAPTER 9

OVERCOMING SOCIAL ANXIETY

Imagine standing in a room full of people, each engaged in lively conversation, while you hover at the fringes, your mind racing with self-doubt. You would like to join in, to share in the laughter and camaraderie, but a voice in your head holds you back. It whispers that you have nothing interesting to say, that others will judge or dismiss you. This internal dialogue is a familiar companion to those grappling with social anxiety, planting seeds of doubt and limiting your ability to connect with others. This chapter aims to transform those whispers into voices of encouragement, guiding you toward a new narrative of confidence and connection.

REFRAMING NEGATIVE THOUGHTS

Recognizing these negative thought patterns is the first step in overcoming their influence. They often manifest as internalized beliefs such as "I'm not interesting" or "People will judge me," they can feel as immovable as the surrounding walls. These thoughts are not truths but reflections of insecurities that have taken root over time. Identifying these beliefs is crucial because it allows you to address them directly rather than letting them operate unchecked in the background. By bringing them into the light, you create an opportunity to challenge their validity and begin the process of change.

Challenging and replacing these negative beliefs with more realistic alternatives is where cognitive restructuring comes into play. This technique, often used in cognitive behavioral therapy, involves questioning the accuracy of your thoughts and developing evidence-based counterarguments. For instance, if your mind insists, "I'm not interesting," pause and ask yourself, "Is this really true?" Reflect on past experiences where you shared a story or idea that captivated others. Use these moments as evidence to counter the negative belief. According to Medical News Today, cognitive restructuring encourages balanced and realistic thinking, which can significantly reduce the impact of unhelpful thinking styles on your well-being. By reframing your thoughts, you shift the narrative from self-doubt to empowerment and confidence.

Practicing self-compassion is another vital strategy in this process. Often, we are our harshest critics, holding ourselves to standards we would never impose on others. Cultivating a compassionate inner dialogue involves treating yourself with the same kindness and understanding you would offer a friend. Start each day with affirmations highlighting your strengths and potential, such as "I am capable of meaningful connections" or "I have valuable insights to share." Complement these affirmations with journaling, where you record positive interactions and moments of connection. This practice reinforces your self-worth and creates a tangible record of your progress and growth.

Cultivating a growth mindset can transform how you perceive social challenges. Instead of viewing them as threats to avoid, see them as opportunities for learning and development. Reflect on past social interactions where you succeeded, no matter how small the victory. Perhaps you initiated a conversation with a stranger or contributed to a group discussion. These successes are stepping stones on your journey to overcoming social anxiety. By focusing on growth rather than perfection, you allow yourself the grace to make mistakes and learn from them, knowing that each experience contributes to your personal development.

Reflection Section: Reframing Thoughts

1. **Identify Negative Thoughts:** Spend a week noting down repetitive negative thoughts related to social interactions. What patterns emerge?
2. **Challenge and Reframe:** Ask, "Is this true for each negative thought? What evidence do I have against it?" Write down more balanced alternatives.
3. **Practice Self-Compassion:** Begin each day with a positive affirmation. Reflect on past interactions and write about moments of connection and growth in your journal.

By embracing these strategies, you gradually dismantle the barriers that social anxiety erects, paving the way for a more confident and connected self.

GRADUAL EXPOSURE TECHNIQUES

Facing social anxiety often feels like standing at the edge of a daunting cliff, but gradual exposure techniques can transform that cliff into a gentle slope. Imagine starting with small, manageable social situations, like attending a friend's dinner party or chatting briefly with a colleague. These low-stakes environments provide a safe space to practice and build confidence. Begin by identifying social situations that trigger mild anxiety. This could be a small gathering or a low-pressure work event. By engaging in these scenarios, you slowly acclimate to the discomfort, reducing its power over you. As you grow more comfortable, you can progressively challenge yourself with higher-stakes interactions, such as speaking up in meetings or attending more significant social events. This incremental approach allows you to confront anxiety without feeling overwhelmed, fostering resilience and self-assurance.

Visualization is a powerful tool to prepare for these exposures, enabling you to rehearse social interactions mentally before they happen. Picture yourself entering a room, greeting people with a smile, and engaging in conversations with ease. Imagine encountering setbacks, like an awkward silence, and handling them calmly and gracefully. Visualization helps desensitize your mind to potential stressors, reducing anxiety when the actual moment arrives. This mental rehearsal builds confidence and creates a sense of familiarity with the situation, making it easier to navigate. By visualizing success, you prime your mind for positive outcomes, reinforcing your ability to manage social challenges effectively.

Tracking your progress is crucial in this process. Maintain a log of your social experiences, noting what worked well and areas for improvement. Reflect on each interaction, celebrating small victories and acknowledging the courage it took to participate. This record serves as a tangible testament to your growth, offering encouragement on days when anxiety feels particularly overwhelming. Adjust your exposure plan as needed, focusing on areas that require more practice or exploring new challenges as your confidence grows. By documenting your journey, you gain insight into patterns and triggers, empowering you to make informed adjustments to your approach.

Celebrating small wins is an integral part of overcoming social anxiety. Each completed exposure task, no matter how minor it may seem, is a step forward. Reward yourself for these achievements, whether indulging in a favorite treat, taking time for a hobby, or simply acknowledging your progress with pride. These celebrations reinforce positive behavior, motivating you to continue pushing boundaries and embracing new social opportunities. By recognizing and valuing each success, you cultivate a positive mindset that views challenges as opportunities for growth rather than obstacles to avoid. This shift in perspective empowers you to approach social interactions with curiosity and confidence, transforming anxiety into a catalyst for personal development.

Interactive Element: Creating Your Exposure Plan

1. **Identify Low-Stakes Scenarios:** List social situations that provoke mild anxiety.
2. **Visualize Success:** Spend a few minutes each day picturing positive outcomes in these scenarios.
3. **Track Progress:** Keep a journal of your experiences, noting successes and areas for adjustment.
4. **Celebrate Achievements:** Plan a small reward for each completed exposure task, reinforcing your progress.

With patience and persistence, gradual exposure techniques can demystify social anxiety, revealing a path toward meaningful connections and enriching interactions.

BUILDING SOCIAL COMFORT ZONES

Creating environments where you feel supported is a cornerstone of overcoming social anxiety. It starts with identifying people and places that naturally put you at ease. Picture moments with friends who accept you without judgment, those who create a sense of belonging with their laughter and understanding glances. These are your supportive allies. Seek out groups or communities that share your interests, like a book club or a local sports team, where the shared activity can naturally foster connection. Hosting small gatherings at your home can also help. These settings allow you to control the environment, choose familiar spaces, and invite trusted individuals. This control can significantly reduce anxiety, creating a safe haven for social practice. By surrounding yourself with supportive people and familiar settings, you lay a solid foundation from which to expand your comfort zone.

Once you establish your safe spaces, consider how you might gradually step beyond them to build confidence. Start by initiating brief conversations with acquaintances, perhaps a colleague you see in the break room or a neighbor you often pass by. These interactions don't need to be profound—sometimes, a simple greeting or question about their day can open the door to deeper connections over time. At work or school, look for group activities where you can participate without the pressure of being the center of attention. Whether joining a team project or attending a workshop, these opportunities allow you to engage with others in a structured setting, reducing the unpredictability that often fuels anxiety. As you participate in such activities, you incrementally expand your comfort zone, learning to navigate new social landscapes with increasing ease.

In unfamiliar settings, finding anchor points can significantly ease anxiety. These are elements or people that provide a sense of familiarity amidst the unknown. Imagine walking into a bustling conference room, scanning faces until you spot a friendly one—a colleague you've worked with or someone who shares your interests. Approaching them can be your first step in acclimating to the environment. Similarly, identifying common interests is another effective strategy. Maybe there's a shared hobby or a mutual acquaintance that can serve as a conversational starting point. These familiar touchstones can ground you, offering stability and reducing the overwhelming nature of new social settings. With anchor points, the unfamiliar becomes less daunting, allowing you to engage more freely.

Reflecting on your growth is crucial in expanding your comfort zones. Take time to assess your progress regularly, noting how your comfort levels have shifted over time. What once seemed intimidating might now feel manageable or even enjoyable. This self-assessment helps you recognize the strides you've made, reinforcing your capability to handle social interactions. Consider keeping a journal where you document these experiences, noting specific moments where you felt more at ease or took a risk that paid off. Reflecting on these instances boosts your confidence and highlights areas where you might want to focus more effort. By acknowledging your growth, you cultivate a mindset that embraces change and encourages further exploration. This ongoing introspection becomes a powerful tool, guiding you toward continued personal development in social settings.

MINDSET SHIFTS FOR ANXIETY REDUCTION

In the whirlwind of social interactions, it's easy to fall into the trap of harsh judgment—both of yourself and others. This tendency often amplifies anxiety, making every conversation feel like a performance with the potential for failure. Adopting a nonjudgmental attitude can transform how you experience these interactions. Recognize that everyone harbors imperfections, and no one is immune to moments of awkwardness or uncertainty. When you let go of the need for judgment, you create space for empathy and understanding. Embracing this mindset involves practicing mindfulness, which encourages staying present and observing thoughts without immediate reaction. By grounding yourself in the present, you can let go of preconceived notions and engage with others more openly, allowing authentic connections to flourish.

Focusing on the present moment can significantly reduce anxiety about future interactions. This approach involves grounding techniques that anchor you to the here and now, pulling you away from the spiraling thoughts of what might happen. Imagine sitting in a meeting, your mind racing with worries about saying the wrong thing. By redirecting your attention to the surrounding sensations—the chair's weight and the rhythm of your breath—you shift your focus to the present. This mindful awareness interrupts the anxiety loop, freeing you from the grip of future concerns. Techniques like deep breathing or the five senses exercise can help center you in the moment, allowing you to engage more fully in conversations without the burden of anticipation.

Accepting uncertainty and imperfection as inherent aspects of social interaction is another powerful mindset shift. Often, the fear of not meeting some imagined standard of perfection paralyzes us, leading to anxiety and avoidance. However, social interactions are inherently unpredictable, and perfection is an unrealistic expectation. Embrace the idea that mistakes and missteps are part of the human experience, offering opportunities for learning and growth. When you let go of the need for flawless performance, you free yourself to participate more genuinely. This acceptance fosters resilience, allowing you to navigate social situations more efficiently and authentically. By viewing imperfections as natural, you can approach interactions with a sense of curiosity and openness rather than fear and self-doubt.

Reframing social scenarios positively is about shifting your perspective from seeing interactions as potential pitfalls to viewing them as opportunities for connection. This change in outlook can transform how you engage with others. Instead of fixating on what could go wrong, focus on each interaction's possibilities. Consider how each conversation is a chance to learn something new, share a piece of yourself, or build meaningful connections. This positive reinterpretation encourages you to approach social situations with enthusiasm rather than apprehension. When you view interactions as opportunities rather than threats, you open yourself to the richness of human connection, allowing anxiety to recede and genuine engagement to take its place.

EMPOWERMENT THROUGH PRACTICE

Imagine waking up with a plan, a commitment to engage with the world just a little more than you did yesterday. Consistent practice is a cornerstone in reducing social anxiety. It's about creating a rhythm of engagement, where social activities become a natural part of your routine rather than an exception. Schedule regular outings, perhaps a weekly coffee meet-up with a friend or a monthly book club. Though seemingly small, these events build a strong foundation of social confidence over time. The more you immerse yourself in these settings, the more familiar and less daunting they become. You start to notice that the anxiety that once felt insurmountable begins to lose its hold, replaced by a growing sense of ease and spontaneity.

Role-playing offers another avenue for development, providing a safe space to practice social skills before stepping into real-world situations. Gather with friends and simulate challenging scenarios, such as introducing yourself at a networking event or striking up small talk with a stranger. This playful yet practical exercise allows you to experiment with different approaches, receive immediate feedback, and build confidence in a low-pressure environment. Rehearsing interactions helps demystify them, breaking down the fear of the unknown. Over time, these rehearsals translate into more fluent and natural conversations when it matters most. Think of role-playing as a rehearsal for life, a way to refine your social tools in a supportive setting.

Feedback is a powerful catalyst for growth, and seeking it from trusted individuals can provide invaluable insights into your social interactions. Ask friends or family members for their honest impressions of your social skills. They might notice habits you're unaware of, or they may highlight strengths you hadn't recognized. This feedback can illuminate areas for improvement and affirm your progress, providing a balanced perspective on your social abilities. Support from others guides your development and reinforces the connections you've built, reminding you that you're not alone in this journey. Embracing constructive criticism with an open mind can lead to profound personal growth, turning perceived weaknesses into opportunities for enhancement.

Documenting and reflecting on your experiences is a practice that deepens self-awareness and tracks progress. Consider keeping a journal dedicated to your social interactions, where you record successes, challenges, and lessons learned. Writing about these experiences helps solidify them in your memory, allowing you to process emotions and extract insights. Reflect on what went well and what could be improved, and celebrate your successes, no matter how small they may seem. Over time, this journal becomes a narrative of your growth, a tangible reminder of the strides you've made. It serves as both a motivational tool and a resource for reflection, offering clarity and encouragement on days when doubt creeps in.

Remember that progress is not always linear as you engage in these practices. There will be days of triumph and days of struggle, but each contributes to your development. Embrace the setbacks as learning opportunities, knowing that each interaction, whether successful or challenging, adds to your arsenal of social skills. With time and consistent effort, you'll find that social anxiety loses its grip, replaced by a newfound confidence and a deepened ability to connect.

Building this foundation empowers you and opens doors to more prosperous, more meaningful interactions. As we transition to the next chapter, we'll explore how these skills translate into professional settings, enhancing personal relationships and career opportunities.

CHAPTER 10

CONTINUOUS GROWTH AND APPLICATION

Picture this: you're sitting in a bustling coffee shop, eavesdropping on fragments of conversations—a manager negotiating a project deadline, a group of friends planning a weekend getaway, and a newcomer nervously introducing themselves to a community group. Each interaction, though unique, offers a glimpse into the tapestry of human communication. This chapter bridges the gap between theory and practice, offering a chance to apply the strategies you've learned in real-world settings. Through practical scenarios, case study analysis, and personal reflection, you'll discover how to transform daily interactions into opportunities for growth. The goal is to help you cultivate an intuitive understanding of communication so it becomes as natural as breathing.

Let's explore workplace scenarios where effective communication is the linchpin of success. Imagine you're in a team meeting discussing a new project. The stakes are high, and tensions can run even higher. How do you navigate this environment with confidence and clarity? Drawing from the communication techniques we've covered, you could start by actively listening and paying close attention to your colleagues' ideas and concerns. This shows respect and allows you to gather diverse perspectives before responding. When it's your turn to speak, structure your points clearly and concisely, emphasizing key ideas with supportive gestures. This helps convey your message and demonstrates leadership, encouraging others to engage and collaborate.

Now, imagine you're at a networking event. The room buzzes with chatter, yet you feel a familiar knot of anxiety. Here is where your newfound skills in initiating and maintaining conversations come to life. Start with an icebreaker— something simple yet engaging, like commenting on the event's atmosphere or asking about recent trends in the field. As the conversation unfolds, employ active listening to show genuine interest, echoing key points to build rapport. These strategies transform an intimidating situation into manageable and meaningful interactions, where connections are forged and opportunities abound.

To deepen our understanding, let's examine some case studies of great communicators who have navigated complex social landscapes. Take, for instance, the eloquence of Martin Luther King Jr., whose speeches convey powerful messages and inspire collective action through vivid imagery and emotive language. Or consider Abraham Lincoln, who mastered the art of brevity, delivering impactful speeches with few words yet profound meaning. These leaders teach us the importance of aligning verbal and nonverbal communication to resonate with diverse audiences. By studying their approaches, you can glean insights into crafting your own style and adapting techniques to suit your personality and objectives.

Reflecting on everyday interactions is crucial for identifying learning opportunities. Think about a casual conversation you had today. What worked well, and where did you stumble? Perhaps you noticed a moment when your body language contradicted your words, or you missed an opportunity to ask a thoughtful follow-up question. These observations are gold mines for growth. They highlight areas for improvement and provide a roadmap for future interactions. Seek feedback from trusted colleagues or friends after meetings or social events. This external perspective can unveil blind spots and reinforce positive habits, supporting your journey toward becoming a more effective communicator.

Theory is invaluable, but the real magic happens when you translate it into practice. Consider role-playing scenarios based on the case studies we've explored. Imagine delivering a speech with King's passion or engaging an audience with Lincoln's brevity. As you rehearse, focus on aligning your verbal messages with nonverbal cues, ensuring your body language reinforces your words. Developing personal strategies using learned techniques allows you to hone your skills in a safe environment before applying them in real-world situations. This practice builds confidence, enabling you to approach each interaction with authenticity and poise.

Interactive Exercise: Practicing Real-World Scenarios

1. **Scenario Selection:** Choose a real-world scenario you often encounter, such as workplace negotiations or networking events.

2. **Role-play:** Act out the scenario with a partner or in front of a mirror, focusing on integrating the communication strategies discussed.
3. **Feedback Loop:** Record the role-play session, then review it to identify strengths and areas for improvement.
4. **Apply and Reflect:** Implement the refined strategies in your next real-world interaction. Reflect on the experience, noting what felt natural and what still needs adjustment.

The journey to becoming a skilled communicator is ongoing and woven into the fabric of daily life. Each interaction is an opportunity to refine your craft and connect with others in meaningful ways. Embrace these moments not as challenges but as stepping stones on the path to personal and professional fulfillment.

Self-Assessment and Reflection

Picture yourself standing at the edge of a reflective pool, peering into its depths. The surface mirrors your image, but beneath it lies a world of insight waiting to be explored. This metaphor captures the essence of self-assessment, an ongoing process where you evaluate your communication skills, track your progress and uncover areas ripe for growth. Just as an artist reviews their canvas to decide the next brushstroke, you also must periodically step back and assess your communication landscape. This exercise isn't about finding fault but discovering potential and celebrating progress.

Begin by creating a checklist of key communication skills you wish to refine. Include active listening, clarity in speech, or the ability to engage others with empathy. As you tick off each item, take a moment to self-rate your effectiveness in each area. Use a simple scale from one to ten to quantify your performance. This tangible measure provides a baseline from which you can monitor improvement. Regular self-assessments help you identify patterns—both strengths to amplify and weaknesses to address—offering a clear map of your communicative journey.

Setting personal development goals is your compass in this exploration. Imagine these goals as destinations on your map, each one guiding you toward enhanced communication. Goals should be specific and measurable, transforming aspirations into achievable targets. You may aim to improve small talk skills by engaging in three new conversations each week. Or you might set a long-term goal to deliver a presentation confidently by year's end. Defining short-term and long-term objectives creates a structured path for growth, ensuring that each step forward is deliberate and meaningful.

Reflecting on past interactions offers a treasure trove of insights and lessons. Consider a recent conversation that left a lasting impression. What about it resonated with you? Was it the ease of dialogue, the connection felt, or a particular challenge you overcame? Journaling these impactful conversations lets you capture fleeting moments of success and lessons learned. Document outcomes, noting what worked and where improvements could be made. As you revisit these reflections, patterns emerge, revealing areas of strength and opportunities for growth. This habit of reflection transforms experience into wisdom, equipping you with the knowledge to navigate future interactions with greater skill.

Feedback from others is a powerful tool for growth, offering perspectives that enhance your self-awareness. Seek input from mentors, peers, or even friends who can provide honest, constructive feedback. Their observations might highlight strengths you had yet to notice or gently point out areas needing attention. When receiving feedback, approach it open-mindedly, viewing criticism as a stepping stone rather than a setback. Constructive criticism is not a reflection of failure but an opportunity to refine and evolve. Integrating this feedback enriches your communication toolkit, enhancing your ability to connect and engage with authenticity.

Imagine feedback as a mirror held up by those around you, reflecting aspects of your communication you might not readily see. Their insights can illuminate blind spots, revealing habits or tendencies that may hinder your effectiveness. This external perspective is invaluable, offering clarity and direction in your pursuit of growth. By welcoming feedback, you invite a collaborative process of development where the wisdom and experience of others support your journey.

In this reflective process, remember that growth is continuous and evolving. Your communication skills are like a garden, requiring regular care and attention to flourish. As you assess, set goals, reflect, and integrate feedback, you nurture this garden, cultivating a vibrant landscape of connection and understanding. Each interaction becomes a chance to learn and grow, a testament to your commitment to becoming a more effective and empathetic communicator. The journey of self-assessment and reflection is not a destination but a lifelong path of discovery, where each step reveals new possibilities and deeper connections.

JOINING COMMUNITIES FOR SUPPORT

Imagine stepping into a room filled with people who share your passion for improving communication. There's an energy in the air, a sense of camaraderie that comes from a shared goal. This is the power of joining communities dedicated to enhancing communication skills. Local speaking clubs or workshops offer a supportive environment where you can practice and refine your abilities. These gatherings are more than just a place to learn—they're a space to connect with others on a similar path. You'll find encouragement and constructive feedback from people who understand the nuances of effective communication. As you interact, you'll pick up tips and techniques not in textbooks but shared generously by those who've faced similar challenges and triumphs.

The digital age has opened up a wealth of opportunities to connect with like-minded individuals online. Social media groups and forums dedicated to communication provide a platform for sharing experiences, seeking advice, and celebrating successes. These virtual spaces are alive with discussions, where members exchange insights on everything from overcoming stage fright to crafting persuasive arguments. You can join conversations at your own pace, contribute when you feel ready, and learn from the diverse perspectives of others. The beauty of these communities lies in their accessibility; you can tap into a global network of support without leaving your home.

Peer learning is a powerful tool for growth. Through collaborative learning sessions and peer-led discussion groups, you engage in the kind of active participation that deepens understanding. These settings encourage dialogue, allowing you to explore different viewpoints and challenge your assumptions. As you share your experiences and techniques, you reinforce your knowledge and gain new insights from others. This exchange of ideas fosters a sense of belonging and mutual respect, creating an environment where learning flourishes. Engaging with peers and striving to enhance their communication skills builds a supportive network that motivates and inspires everyone's continued improvement.

Networking with individuals who share your communication goals can open doors to new opportunities and experiences. Attending networking events and conferences exposes you to a community of professionals who are passionate about effective communication. These gatherings are not just about exchanging business cards but about forming genuine connections with people who can offer guidance, mentorship, and collaboration. Building relationships with communication coaches or trainers can provide personalized insights and feedback, helping you refine your skills and achieve your objectives. These mentors can offer a fresh perspective, helping you navigate the complexities of communication with more confidence and clarity.

Participating in communication challenges and competitions is an excellent way to test and refine your skills in a real-world setting. Public speaking contests offer a platform to practice delivering messages with clarity and impact. These events push you out of your comfort zone, encouraging you to apply what you've learned under pressure. Debating clubs and events provide another avenue for honing your ability to construct arguments and engage in persuasive dialogue. These competitive environments foster resilience, teaching you to think on your feet and adapt to unexpected challenges. The experience gained from participating in these activities is invaluable, equipping you with the skills needed to excel in various communication contexts.

Engaging with communities, whether in-person or online, is vital to continuous growth. These networks offer support, inspiration, and a wealth of knowledge that enriches your journey toward becoming a more effective communicator. Through these interactions, you gain practical insights, build meaningful connections, and cultivate a sense of belonging within a community of like-minded individuals. So, take the plunge—join a club, participate in a forum, attend a conference, or enter a competition. The relationships and experiences you gain will be invaluable, propelling you toward your communication goals with renewed vigor and enthusiasm.

RESOURCES FOR LIFELONG LEARNING

Imagine standing on the shore of a vast ocean of knowledge, where each wave brings new insights and understanding. This is the realm of lifelong learning—an ongoing adventure that enriches your communication skills and deepens your connection with others. To navigate this expansive sea, let's explore some essential resources that can guide you on your path. Books, articles, podcasts, and courses serve as your compass, offering unique perspectives and techniques to enhance your communication prowess. Delve into recommended reading lists that cover everything from foundational theories to advanced strategies. Titles like *"Crucial Conversations"* and *"The Charisma Myth"* provide practical insights, while journal articles like *Harvard Business Review* offer the latest research and trends. Podcasts such as *"The Communication Guys"* provide engaging discussions that you can listen to during your daily routine. Online courses from platforms like Coursera or LinkedIn Learning offer structured learning experiences, allowing you to deepen your skills at your own pace. These resources are not just repositories of information; they are invitations to continually engage with new ideas and refine your abilities.

In our digital age, technology is an invaluable ally in your learning journey. Imagine having a personal tutor in your pocket, ready to assist you anytime. Apps like Duolingo and Babbel make language learning accessible, offering bite-sized lessons that fit into your day. For those looking to improve their speech, apps like Orai provide feedback on clarity and pace, helping you hone your delivery. Online webinars and virtual workshops bring expert knowledge straight to your home, allowing you to learn from thought leaders without the need for travel. These digital tools break down barriers to education, providing flexible options that accommodate your lifestyle. Whether you have five minutes or an hour, technology ensures that learning is always within reach. Embrace these advancements as tools that empower you to take charge of your growth, transforming moments of downtime into opportunities for development.

Staying informed on communication trends keeps you at the forefront of the field. The communication landscape is ever-evolving, shaped by cultural shifts and technological advancements. Subscribing to communication journals or newsletters ensures you remain updated on the latest research and innovations. Sources like *Communication World* or *NPR's TED Radio Hour* offer insights into emerging theories and practices, while newsletters from platforms like Medium deliver curated content directly to your inbox. By staying informed, you equip yourself with the knowledge to adapt and thrive in a changing world. This proactive approach enhances your skills and positions you as a thought leader who is not just part of the conversation but shaping it.

Engage with these resources regularly, making it a habit to explore new ideas and challenge your assumptions.

Creating a personalized learning plan is a powerful step toward continuous growth. Picture this plan as a map, guiding you through the vast communication landscape. Begin by identifying gaps in your knowledge or skills—areas where you feel less confident or curious to explore further. Perhaps you're eager to develop your storytelling abilities or wish to refine your negotiation tactics. Once you've identified these areas, set specific goals for your learning journey. These goals act as destinations, providing direction and motivating you to stay on course. Schedule regular learning activities, whether it's reading a chapter of a book, attending a webinar, or practicing a new technique. Review your progress periodically, celebrating milestones and adjusting your plan as needed. This personalized approach transforms learning from a passive activity into an active pursuit, one that is tailored to your needs and aspirations.

As we bring this chapter to a close, remember that the path of lifelong learning is not linear but a tapestry of experiences and insights. Each resource, whether a book, app, or conversation, adds a thread to this tapestry, enriching your understanding and expanding your horizons. Embrace the journey with curiosity and openness, knowing that every step you take brings you closer to the communicator you aspire to be. With each lesson learned and skill refined, you empower yourself to navigate the complexities of human connection with confidence and empathy. This commitment to growth is a pursuit of knowledge and a celebration of the human spirit's boundless potential.

KEEPING THE CONVERSATION GOING

Now that you're equipped to talk to anyone with confidence and ease, it's time to help others find their own path to connection.

By leaving a review for *The Power of How to Talk to Anyone* on Amazon, you're guiding future readers to the tools they need to feel comfortable, make new friends, and truly connect. Your honest thoughts can be the encouragement someone else needs to start their journey.

Thank you for keeping the spirit of communication alive. When we share our experiences, we empower others to grow and connect, just like you have.

Scan the QR code below to leave a review:

[https://www.amazon.com/review/review-your-purchases/?asin=BOOKASIN]

Granite Sparks

CONCLUSION

As we reach the end of this journey together, let's revisit the core themes woven throughout this book. We've embarked on a path from the shadows of social anxiety to the bright realm of confident communication. This transformation hinges on embracing authenticity and the profound impact of verbal and nonverbal cues in forging genuine connections. You've learned to transcend initial hesitations, allowing your true self to shine in every interaction.

Throughout our exploration, several key takeaways have emerged. Mindset shifts are a powerful foundation for change, reminding us that growth and learning are lifelong commitments. Active listening and empathy, cornerstones of effective communication, have shown us how to truly engage with others, creating relationships built on understanding and trust. We've delved into the nuances of nonverbal communication, recognizing its silent yet significant role in conveying our intentions and emotions. Navigating difficult conversations and mastering digital interactions have equipped you with the skills necessary to handle any scenario with grace and confidence.

But remember, the journey doesn't end here. Applying these skills in your daily life is where the fundamental transformation occurs. Each conversation is a chance to practice, refine, and master what you've learned. Consistent application will solidify these skills, turning them into second nature. As you continue to engage with others, you'll notice an increase in your confidence and the depth of your connections. Your improved communication skills will open doors to new personal and professional opportunities. This newfound ability to connect with others on a deeper level will enhance your relationships and broaden your horizons.

Still, it's essential to acknowledge that challenges may arise along the way. Communication is an ever-evolving skill, and setbacks are to be expected. Embrace resilience and adaptability as your allies in this journey. Each stumble is an opportunity for growth, learning, and improvement. Don't be discouraged by temporary setbacks; instead, view them as stepping stones toward becoming an even more effective communicator.

With the knowledge and tools you've gained, now is the time for action. Set personal communication goals that align with your aspirations. Join communities that foster growth and support, where you can share your experiences and learn from others. Seek feedback regularly, as it is essential for continuous improvement. Your commitment to growth and development will be the driving force behind your success.

Lifelong learning is a vital aspect of mastering communication. Stay informed about new trends and techniques, and explore additional resources to enhance your skills further. The world of communication is vast and constantly changing, offering endless opportunities for growth and discovery. You'll ensure your skills remain sharp and relevant by remaining curious and open to learning.

As you move forward, remember that every conversation is more than just an exchange of words. It's a chance to connect, to understand, and to grow. You possess the ability to transform your communication skills into a powerful tool for success. Embrace this potential with confidence and courage. With each interaction, you can make a meaningful impact, enriching your life and those around you.

Thank you for allowing me to be a part of your journey. I'm passionate about helping you overcome social anxiety and build genuine connections. Remember that you're never alone in this endeavor. The path to effective communication is filled with opportunities for growth and discovery. Embrace it wholeheartedly, and watch your world expand with newfound confidence and connection.

REFERENCES

Botsplash. (n.d.). The best 10 digital communication strategies to follow in the digital age. Retrieved from https://www.botsplash.com/post/digital-communication-strategies

Comms Creatives. (2022, February 8). The top free online communities for comms pros. Retrieved from https://commscreatives.com/2022/02/08/comms-communities-online/

Discovery ADR. (n.d.). How important are first impressions in the workplace? Retrieved from https://www.discovery-adr.com/how-important-are-first-impressions-in-the-workplace/

Europarc. (n.d.). 10 strategies for overcoming language barriers. Retrieved from https://www.europarc.org/communication-skills/pdf/10%20Strategies%20for%20Overcoming%20Language%20Barriers.pdf

Gaffney, S. (n.d.). Lessons from great communicators. Retrieved from https://stevengaffney.com/lessons-from-great-communicators/

HelpGuide. (n.d.). Body language and nonverbal communication.Retrieved from https://www.helpguide.org/relationships/communication/nonverbal-communication

HubSpot. (n.d.). 157 of the best email subject lines we've ever seen. Retrieved from https://blog.hubspot.com/marketing/best-email-subject-lines-list

Indeed. (n.d.). 17 effective icebreaker activities for groups of adults. Retrieved from https://ca.indeed.com/career-advice/career-development/icebreaker-activities-for-adults

Kammeyer, J. (n.d.). Growth mindset improves communication. Retrieved from https://jenniferkammeyer.com/growth-mindset-improves-communication/

Kilpatrick Executive Search. (n.d.). How cultural diversity affects business communication. Retrieved from https://www.kilpatrickexecutive.com/news/how-cultural-diversity-affects-business-communication/

MindTools. (n.d.). The situation-behavior-impact™ feedback tool. Retrieved from https://www.mindtools.com/ay86376/the-situation-behavior-impact-feedback-tool

Morin, A. (2016, October 22). There is a clear line between oversharing and being authentic: Here's how to avoid crossing it. Forbes. Retrieved from https://www.forbes.com/sites/amymorin/2016/10/22/there-is-a-clear-line-between-oversharing-and-being-authentic-heres-how-to-avoid-crossing-it/

Ninety.io. (n.d.). Why communication in the workplace is critical for success. Retrieved from https://www.ninety.io/blog/why-communication-in-the-workplace-is-critical-for-success

Oxford Research Encyclopedia of Psychology. (n.d.). Mirror neurons, empathy, and the other. Retrieved from https://oxfordre.com/psychology/display/10.1093/acrefore/9780190236557.001.0001/acrefore-9780190236557-e-605

Paulekman.com. (n.d.). Micro expressions | Facial expressions. Retrieved from https://www.paulekman.com/resources/micro-expressions/

Pumble. (n.d.). 18 business communication trends for 2024 and beyond. Retrieved from https://pumble.com/blog/communication-trends/

Psychology Today. (2014). How self-awareness leads to effective communication. Retrieved from https://www.psychologytoday.com/us/blog/turning-point/201404/how-self-awareness-leads-effective-communication

United Language Group. (n.d.). Communicating in high context vs. low context cultures. Retrieved from https://www.unitedlanguagegroup.com/learn/communicating-high-context-vs-low-context-cultures

Verywell Mind. (n.d.). 7 active listening techniques for better communication. Retrieved from https://www.verywellmind.com/what-is-active-listening-3024343

9 798348 318635